Backyard Ice Rink

THE COUNTRYMAN PRESS

A division of W. W. Norton & Company

Independent Publishers Since 1923

Backyard Ice Rink

A Step-by-Step Guide for
Building Your Own
Hockey Rink at Home

JOE
PROULX

COUNTRY
MAN
KNOW
HOW

THE COUNTRYMAN PRESS
www.countrymanpress.com

A division of W. W. Norton & Company, Inc.
500 Fifth Avenue, New York, NY 10110
www.wwnorton.com

978-1-58157-299-5 (pbk.)

10 9 8 7 6 5 4 3 2 1

DEDICATION

To my dad, the best unpaid employee money can buy.
Our November weeks together are something I will forever cherish.

To RJ, Reese, and Ryder, for laughing loud enough while you skate that the rink
gods hear and keep it cold. Thanks for keeping the secret from mom
that I only build the rink for you guys.

And to Meaghan, for holding down the fort and fully supporting me while I live
out my childish dreams and act on my impulses. And for insisting that any
house we buy have a spot for a rink.

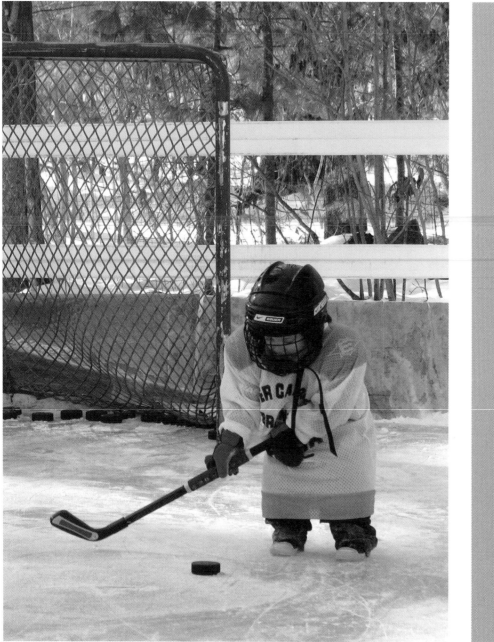

CONTENTS

FOREWORD: OUR BACKYARD RINK:
A LOVE STORY, BY BRIAN FALLA 9

INTRODUCTION 13

CHAPTER ONE:
FIVE REASONS WHY YOU SHOULD
BUILD A BACKYARD RINK 17

CHAPTER TWO:
RINK-BUILDING FAQS 31

CHAPTER THREE:
GETTING STARTED 51
How to Determine the Slope of Your Yard . . . 59
How to Square Up and Prep Your
    Rink Site for Construction 65

CHAPTER FOUR:
BUILDING YOUR RINK 71
Rink Plan 1: The $250 Rink 72
Rink Plan 2: The 2"× 12"+ Rebar Rink 77
Rink Plan 3: The Nicerink System 81
Rink Plan 4: The Full Dasher Boards Rink . . 86
Fill Day! When and How to Lay the Liner
    and Fill Your Rink 93

CHAPTER FIVE:
MAINTAINING YOUR RINK 99
How to Make Your Own Ice
    Thickness Ruler 107

CHAPTER SIX:
DISASSEMBLING YOUR RINK 113

CHAPTER SEVEN:
CUSTOMIZING (AND ENJOYING)
YOUR RINK .121
How to Build an Official US Pond
    Hockey Goal 122
How to Build a $20 Rink Bench 126
How to Build a PVC Skating Aid 131
Backyard Rink Activities 135

RESOURCES 141

GLOSSARY 142

ACKNOWLEDGMENTS 145

INDEX 149

Our Backyard Rink: A Love Story

by Brian Falla

Every year of my childhood, when the first breaths of winter reached our New England home, my heart began to swell. Our backyard rink was my family's beloved cold weather companion, warming our souls, pulling in friends, and knitting us closer together.

It sounds like hyperbole to suggest that this structure of plywood, plastic, and ice was treated as a living, breathing relation, but it was very much a branch on our family tree. Its birth each winter was met with much anticipation and joy; its death each spring mourned with great sorrow. We discussed its health volubly at the dinner table. We inspected the newest ten-day forecast as if it were a loved one's EKG readings. The rink connected us in ways that otherwise seemed impossible.

When my father originally built the rink in 1981, he did so largely to create a place for my sister and me to skate. In his mind, the rink provided available ice when the ponds were either covered in snow or otherwise rendered unskateable. But in all our lives, the rink's ultimate role far surpassed merely giving us a place to skate.

For my dad, who wrote a popular book about backyard hockey called *Home Ice*, it became a great connector not only to his kids, but also to friends and family who would flock to the rink every winter. As the years went on and his own ice time diminished, the rink's role in his life expanded. It suddenly became a lens through which to view his children growing up.

The rink was probably our family's sole shared

passion, and it was unquestionably the place we spent the bulk of our time together. When winter unleashed its wrath and buried us in mounds of white, the four of us would trudge out with our shovels—because my father had Luddite tendencies, we did not own a snow blower until into well into the 2000s—and begin merrily clearing the ice.

As I grew into a diffident teen and the conversational landscape with my parents became more barren, the rink became our safe haven: a place where we could talk about life's problems, no matter how difficult.

Looking back, my most cherished memories were not the weekend all-day pick-up games or the parties but the moments with family.

A few months after my father died, I spent a night clearing a recent snowfall and resurfacing the rink with the garden hose. Orion twinkled on my right wing, the Sea of Tranquility on my left. The only sounds were the soft trickle of the water as it spread across the ice and an occasional bass note from an expansion crack. Looking up at the sky, I imagined my father gazing down and smiling. I wiped a tear off my cheek.

If you ever happen upon a backyard rink person whistling down the street at the prospect of an early arctic blast, or mourning over a spring thaw, please be aware: they are not insane.

They are just in love.

Introduction

Standing for the first time on the first backyard rink that I had built as an adult, I took a mental snapshot and tried to breathe in the experience. It was Christmas morning. In my arms I held my two-year-old firstborn son, his Bauer-clad feet swinging wildly on the ice. My dad stood rinkside, his smile as big and proud as it must have been twenty-five years earlier. My wife took photos from the deck, finally understanding why her crazy husband had talked her into buying all that wood and giant liner.

I took a deep breath and exhaled. We had a rink in our backyard, and the most important people in my world were enjoying it.

"It'll be hard," the naysayers warned. "You'll need to shovel all the snow," they said. "It's expensive!" they cautioned. I knew. But I didn't care. All I knew was that putting a rink in our yard would be amazing and memorable, and already in those first five minutes on Christmas morning in 2008, I was right. We were a backyard rink family.

It's been nearly seven years since that day, and in that time the rink has been as big a part of our family as any living, breathing member. It's hosted large weekend skating parties and solo stress-relief sessions under the stars. Perhaps most importantly, all three of my children have experienced the "holy-cow-I'm-doing-it" excitement that comes with their first unassisted steps on frozen water. All on our little backyard rink.

Along the way I started writing about my rink

experiences on www.backyard-hockey.com. What started as a blog to host pictures of my kids skating has grown to become one of the most popular outdoor-hockey websites in the world. We now have a growing message-board area where both new and veteran rink builders can share ideas and ask questions, and pictures of smiling kids clad in skates and helmets reinforce the community approach we've strived to build.

In 2011, emboldened by several years of rink lessons learned, my wife and I launched Elite Backyard Rinks, a New Hampshire–based company that builds backyard rinks for people who may not necessarily have the time or desire to build one themselves. In our four seasons of existence, we've built more than eighty backyard rinks of all shapes and sizes, helping to bring the awesomeness of backyard rinks to families across New Hampshire and Massachusetts.

The world of backyard rink building is about welcoming a special kind of experience not found anywhere else in the world. It's about sacrificing hours of your Friday night to shoveling snow so that the rink is ready for the kids Saturday morning. It means embracing temps in the teens and twenties, cursing the thirties and forties, and turning an unused piece of your barren, snow-covered yard into a venue for exploration, growth, and laughter. It's about scoring the winning goal in Game 7 of the Stanley Cup Finals, often several times in one day.

This book was written to share those experiences and our expertise with a wider audience and to see to it that as many families as possible experience the wonder of the backyard rink. So read on, absorb the nuts and bolts of our instructional posts, digest our rink passion, and go build your rink.

CHAPTER ONE

Five Reasons Why You Should Build a Backyard Rink

Selling the idea of a backyard rink to your kids is a piece of cake. It's the other people in your life that may pose a challenge. Not everyone sees right away the benefits and perks of having a rink in your yard, and you're almost certainly going to have to campaign for it that first season. So before you turn the page to the how-to plans, I want to ignite your passion for backyard rink building, the very reason why you picked up this book in the first place, and help you build a case for that rink. There are dozens of reasons to build a backyard rink. But we'll start with five.

Reason #1: It's not nearly as hard or expensive as you think it is

I know the feeling: You show up to a friend's house, and there are a dozen people tooling around on his rink, laughing and ringing pucks off the sturdy boards. There's a table full of hot cocoa and cookies, the lights are blazing, the music's on, and everything seems too coordinated and well set up. "This is *amazing*," you think to yourself. "But there's no way I could pull this off."

Allow me to let you in on a little secret: Once upon a time, your gracious host stood in the lumber aisle at Home Depot with a crude drawing in his left hand and a calculator in his right. And he questioned the hell out of his sanity (as did his wife). Maybe he left and drove home, only to return the next day. Maybe he built his rink once, and an entire wall fell down, and he had to put it back together. My point is that all people started out somewhere, and with each passing year, they gained a little bit more knowledge and a little bit more confidence until they built the beauty you showed up to skate on.

Besides, you're holding in your hands a book that will answer every single question you might have, and that will provide you with step-by-step directions to build a rink with a bunch of parts you can find at any hardware store! Intimidating? Maybe at first. But too difficult to even try? Hardly.

At its most basic level, a backyard rink is simply a crude, shallow aboveground pool—you have your walls, your supports, and your liner to hold the water. That's all a rink is.

As for price, the plans you'll find later in this book cater to several different price ranges. The first rink I ever built—the one that my oldest son learned to skate on—was built using the cheapest plywood I could find and came in at under $250. (You can read the details of this build on page 72.) Sure, it wasn't going to win any beauty pageants, but what I learned in those first few winters about building rinks and maintaining the ice allowed me to build a bigger and better rink with confidence. If money's no object, then there are some great rink-specific parts companies out there who would love to talk to you. But it's not a prerequisite that you spend $2,000 on a rink. Not even close.

Reason #2: You'll be the hero of the neighborhood

What burgers on the grill are to summer, backyard rinks are to winter. Once you drop in the liner and fill up your rink, your friends and neighbors will flock to its glossy, untarnished wonderfulness. In a day and age where parents sit in their warm cars at bus stops to avoid conversation, there is something friendly and inviting about a backyard rink. Perhaps it's the novelty. Or maybe the mother of four across the street just wants her kids to offload some energy before bedtime. But regardless of what exactly it is that people find so fascinating about your backyard rink, the reality is that it's a conversation piece, and one that quite often leads to a few beers around the fire while the kids play around on the ice. And just like that, new friendships are made. Happens all the time.

And if your kids are older, or if you're already friendly with your neighbors and their kids, it's even better. "Maaaaa, I'm booooored" will be a thing of the past! Entire weekends will be spent on the rink. You'll invest in a small fire pit, your friends will bring the hot chocolate and brownies, and entire weekends will melt away as you sit rinkside, beverage in hand, gossiping about next year's teacher assignments. Or, perhaps more likely, you'll finally be able to cook dinner in peace with all the kids outside for the afternoon. Either way, the rink will serve as a de facto winter sandlot, and your kids and their friends will be better off for it.

Reason #3: You'll be making magic and memories

Think back to your childhood and to some of your happiest memories. For me, one of my most vivid recollections was a day of hockey with my peewee team on a local pond, which just happened to be across the street from the house of one of my team-mates. I live about two miles from that pond now, and when I drive by, I can still remember where we shoveled out a rink, put the nets, and ate the incredibly delicious peanut-butter-chocolate fudge one of the parents brought. We must have played for six hours, and I imagine most of us whined when told we had to leave. It was just one of those magical, perfect days, the ones that stick with you for eternity.

And do you know what's great? When you build a backyard rink, you're manufacturing memories for your kids and their friends. They won't realize it when they're skating, and probably not for years after. But someday, they'll look back, and the rink will be central to some of their happiest moments.

The late, great Jack Falla, author of several hockey books, Boston University professor, and builder of a backyard rink for nearly thirty years, put it best in an email to a group of backyard rink builders: "I wish you all well with your rinks. Keep them going as long as you can. Everyone who skates

on those rinks will remember it. And will remember you. I suppose in that way a rink confers a kind of immortality."

His son Brian, now grown with children of his own, offered his own thoughts. "As tweenies and teenies, my sister and I weren't the greatest of companions around the dinner table every night and conversational topics were sparse. But we could talk about the rink. It was our own conversational safe haven, and possibly the lone passion shared by all four of us. And get the four of us out on the rink, be it skating or shoveling out after another winter storm, and we came together with a closeness that was absent from other arenas. Conversations were easier, jokes funnier, rebukes less stinging, personal questions less probing (and if you really took offense, you could always throw the next puck in the offender's corner and settle it the old-fashioned way). The rink was, in our house at least, the only thing that could effectively bridge the parent–child generational chasm."

Sure, rinks are just wood and plastic and water. But there's something special about that combination that brings out the best in people. So build a rink now, and watch as the memories are made.

Reason #4: A rink is a secret skill-builder

Stanley Kaplan, the man behind the test prep company, once said, "Repetition breeds familiarity. Familiarity breeds confidence. Confidence breeds success."

He was undoubtedly talking about long division or comma usage or some other thing that would undoubtedly make me sleepy, but his quote lends itself to many other pursuits—hockey included.

Now before I go too far, let me issue a stern warning: If you are reading this book and planning on building a backyard rink so that Little Jimmy can

make it to the NHL, please stop. Put this book down, go back to the bookstore or library, and exchange it for a parenting guide for raising children with reasonable and fair expectations. Okay? Okay.

That said, there's nothing wrong with wanting to improve your own skills or providing your children with a venue where they can improve theirs. Kids have a natural desire to improve and learn, perhaps trumped only by their desire to have fun, and a rink gives them the opportunity to do both.

For younger skaters, it can be intimidating to learn to skate within the confines of a youth hockey program or a public skating session. With dozens of other kids and adults zooming around under bright lights, the focus is less on what they're doing and more on what everyone else seems to be doing so much better. Frustration is common. But on your own rink, the pace at which you introduce them to the art of skating is entirely established by you and your new skater.

For our twins, the first two or three sessions on our rink this past winter (when they were about two years old) consisted of us gearing them up in hockey equipment, holding them up on the rink, then showing them how fun it is to fall down. With the equipment there is no pain or injury, and kids absolutely love falling and sliding around (almost as much as they enjoy watching *you* fall). Only later did they have enough confidence to stand on their own, and eventually to take their first timid footsteps. I can't imagine having been able to ease them into it in the middle of a busy public skating session at the local

rink. In our backyard, we were in complete control, and I think that helped.

For older skaters, it's all about freedom, repetition, and fun. Most hockey players today spend indoor practices either standing in line or watching instruction, then occasionally getting an opportunity to handle the puck, take a shot, or improve on some other skill. Games are even worse, with studies showing that the average player touches the puck a mere twenty seconds over the course of an entire game. Twenty seconds! Put a kid on a backyard rink, and they'll eclipse that within the first minute. See where this is going?

With a rink of their own, the ability to strap on the skates and grab a stick allows instant access to a virtual training playground. With a net and a half-dozen pucks, a hockey player will take more shots and spend more time with the puck on their stick than they will in a month's worth of practices. And given that backyard rinks are novel and fun, hockey-loving kids will improve their game by repetition with smiles on their faces. Want to improve shot accuracy? Hang a few makeshift targets in the top corners of the goal and watch your child and his friends bust one another's chops as they take dozens of shots at them. Want to see an improvement in agility? Grab some cones (or boots or pucks or old sticks) and put together an obstacle course. For added laughter and competition, time the kids with a stopwatch app on your smartphone. The fun will be constant and natural, but the skill-building will be real and tangible.

Reason #5: It's cheaper than a therapist (and look, no copays!)

Much of what has been written in this book talks about a rink's impact on children. And while it's true that your kids will love your rink, and they'll improve their games and build memories while they enjoy it, there's an added benefit for us old folks. Whether we want to admit it or not, pretty much every living, breathing adult could use some time on the leather couch. We're all inundated with stressors: bills, deadlines, work projects, bus schedules, student-loan payments. All of these things swirl around our heads like our own personal tornados, constantly injecting themselves into our thought processes throughout the day. But there's a simple, albeit temporary solution: Put on your skates or boots, grab your stick or hose, and step on the ice.

Many of my ills have been cured (or at least temporarily forgotten) on my backyard rink. Once the kids are asleep and I'm standing at center ice in the dead of night, letting water flow freely from the hose and painting the ice smooth again, it's easy to forget about paying the mortgage or the work presentation at 9 a.m. the next morning. I stare at the trees as they reflect the halogen light back at me and listen to them creak eerily in the breeze. I take in deep breaths of frozen air. All this injects new energy into what can be a relentless and tiring life.

On weekend days, two hours on the rink will do as much good for your mood and your body as any dose of Prozac. That cold burn in the back of your throat will be a welcome reminder of the crisp winter air and the laughter you've shared with your kids. Family two-on-twos will leave you soaked in sweat, exhausted from exertion, and 10,000 miles away from your iPhone. Sure, problems never go away for good, but a mental vacation is never as sweet as it is when accompanied by a stick, a puck, and a sheet of ice.

Hopefully some of these reasons connect with you, and you're ready to continue on to the instructional part of the book. Just as every rink is unique, every rink builder has their own reasons for undertaking what many consider a somewhat insane attempt to tame winter. What's most important is that you know why you're doing it, and that you keep that reason in your back pocket when things get challenging or your coworkers tell you you're nuts. One thing is for certain: it *will* be worth it when the dust settles. That's a promise.

CHAPTER TWO

Rink-Building FAQs

I know where you are mentally: You like the thought of a rink in your yard, and your spouse is finally on board, but you're apprehensive and unsure of where to start. You've talked to dozens of people who have built rinks and their advice is all over the map. The guy at work told you to build it one way, but then the woman at the rink told you to build it a different way. Maybe this rink thing is just too complicated.

Take a deep breath and relax. We can help.

When you set out to build your first rink, you're going to have a lot of questions. And between my five years of writing for backyard-hockey.com and my four years of building rinks for Elite Backyard

Rinks, I've heard most of them. In this chapter, I'll aim to answer them—from questions about ice maitenance to building on a sloped yard to when to fill your rink up with water, the follwing are some basics that we can all agree on.

Won't a rink kill my grass?

Good news! Unless you put your liner down in August or leave it in until May, you'll be fine. The grass in most backyard-rink-friendly areas of the world goes dormant in the winter. When exactly that takes place depends on your climate and the exact species of grass in your yard, but a safe bet is that your grass will go dormant during the month of November and will come out of dormancy in the month of March. As the weather turns colder in November, an early freeze is often enough to send a lawn into dormancy. Once you experience several frigid nights, your grass will be completely dormant and will cease to grow or exhibit vibrant color. We've all had BBQs or parties where someone leaves a cooler or a lawn chair on the grass for a day or two, and it leaves behind a brown patch of dead grass. This is because the grass is still growing, and subsequently in need of sunlight and water. But in winter? The grass hibernates like Yogi Bear himself.

There are two primary steps to the backyard rink construction process: frame construction and liner placement. In my experience, these two steps are often done a week or two apart, and often in late November and early December respectively. With that in mind, it is absolutely possible to jump the gun on the frame install and damage the grass underneath your boards. If you erect the frame with the grass still growing, you may see artifacts of that when everything comes down the following spring. But for the most part, if you wait until you experi-

ence some early frost, you'll be fine. And once you drop the liner in December, the grass under your slab will be completely dormant and will subsequently come back up in March as if the rink had never been there.

The most important step? The spring teardown. My advice is always to drain the rink and get rid of the liner as soon as your ice slab melts. Waiting any longer may jeopardize the grass as it comes out of hibernation, and if you think your spouse is angry when you leave your lawn chair out during the summer, just wait for the wrath when the dead grass is 40' x 60'.

My yard is sloped—can I still build a rink?

First off, I commend you. Most folks think that their yard is laser flat, and so I appreciate that you're already admitting you have a slope issue. As we all know, admitting you have a problem is the first step. But in order to truly answer this question, we need to know exactly how sloped. To do that, follow our instructions in chapter 3 and come back to this section when you know for sure how many inches of water we're talking about.

My general rules:

· Flat to about 8" of depth: perfection

· 9" to 12": You're good, but make sure your bracing is solid and the brackets more than 4' apart

- 12" to 16": Things are getting real, so double up on the bracing (every 2' instead of every 4')

- 16"+: Consult a pro, or change the rink dimensions slightly to bring this number down

You don't need to have a perfectly flat spot for your rink, but after eighty-plus rink builds I can definitely say that the easiest and least stressful rinks also have the least amount of slope. Water is a heavy, powerful beast, and it doesn't want to be confined inside your rink boards. So the least amount of water you need, the easier your rink season will be.

Can I use snowbanks as boards and omit the liner when building my rink?

The short answer? Sure.

The longer answer? Sure, but it's *really* difficult to do unless you have the right climate (think northern Canada). The method I'm most familiar with—and the method we'll be exclusively mentioning in this book—uses boards, some sort of bracket, and a plastic liner. In my New England climate, that works best. You can certainly do it the old-fashioned way by tamping down the snow and spraying it with water until it's smooth, but if you get hit with a few days of 40-degree temps, your rink could literally melt away. With the boards-and-liner approach, you

may lose your ice surface on those warm days, but the water stays put and re-freezes as soon as it's cold again.

What is the best way to build a rink?

I've answered this question for a long time, and I've always given it the same answer: There is no "best way" that fits all. First, everyone's yard is different—with different slopes, features, and landscaping. Next, the budget can range from our entry-level $250 rink to full refrigerated systems that cost more than $25,000, and everywhere in between. There's also the availability of parts, your expertise with certain materials, the importance of aesthetics, and dozens of other factors. After living and breathing the outdoor hockey experience for as long as I have, one of my favorite things is how rinks develop a certain personality, and how each rink is as different and unique as its builder. In the end, we all want to take advantage of the cold weather and be able to skate under the open sky—and whether you use plywood or dimensional lumber, whether you brace with wooden stakes or backyard rink-specific brackets, as long as you're able to skate on it, then in my mind, you've built the best rink for you.

When should I build my rink frame?

The build is actually two steps: the frame install and the liner placement on fill day.

I like to joke on our backyard-hockey.com Facebook page that the day after Thanksgiving in the United States is "National Build Your Rink Frame Day," but there's a reason for that. Late November is typically the perfect combination of mild weather and soft ground (for pounding in your supports), but it's also close enough to those frigid winter temps that you're not staring at your rink frame for months before you can use it. In years when the weather cooperates, we'll finish building all of our customers' rinks right around Thanksgiving, and we'll fill a week or two into December.

Of course, your situation may vary. If you don't mind staring at your boards for a month or more, you could always build the frame in October or early November. The benefit there is that the weather is nicer and you don't risk an unseasonably cold late November that could harden the ground earlier than usual.

There's always that rogue warm weekend in December that gives all of the last-minute rink builders one more chance to get their supports in before the ground freezes for good. But wait until December in a cold year and you could be left with frozen ground and a bunch of useless rink parts, so it's a risk.

For most, November is when the frame goes up, and December is when we fill.

When should I fill my rink?

When it comes to filling a rink, you're looking for these four things, in order of importance:

· The next three to four days should be below 32 °F (0 °C) during the day.

· The next three to four nights should be in the teens and twenties overnight.

· The forecast should call for as little snow as possible (ideally none).

· Wind should be minimal on filling day.

The first two are pretty easy to understand—if you want to skate on water, you need some cold temps to turn it to ice. The best way to make that happen is to fill in advance of a cold snap.

Some of you might argue with the third point, assuming that snow melting into your newly filled rink would make the water freeze more quickly. To a certain point, that might be true. But the risk is that you end up with so much snow that it starts to pile up on top of your not-quite-frozen rink, putting you in a difficult spot. I ran into this with my first-ever attempt. I filled my rink and it formed a thin layer of ice in the first day. But then it snowed . . . and snowed . . . and snowed. After a foot of snow had fallen, I had a rink that couldn't support my weight but needed to be shoveled. It's a difficult situation for sure, so it's best to avoid filling if snow is forecast.

Wind just makes it more difficult to lay the liner down flat. Since we build more than thirty rinks a year for local customers, it's inevitable that we get some wind gusts when laying the liner down. Nothing is more frustrating than a gust of wind turning your rink liner into a boat sail and undoing a half hour of work before your eyes. So while you can't always control it, if you have the option to wait for a calmer day, I'd advise you to do it.

There are a number of websites that will give you a forecast, so find one you trust and check it daily once your frame is built. And if you know other folks in your area who build, keep in touch with them to see what they're doing. Deciding when to fill your rink is an inexact science, but if you follow those four rules as best you can, you set yourself up for a successful start to the rink season.

How much water will I need?

For the next few questions, I'm going to start with the general answer and then dive into the math-nerd answer.

We've built more than eighty rinks since 2011, and I'd say probably seventy-five of them used between 6,000 and 9,000 gallons.

The math-nerd answer depends entirely on the size of your rink and how thick you want your ice slab to be. As a general rule, you're going to want to fill until the shallowest part of your rink has 4" of water in it. This gives the ice enough thickness to support adults standing on it. That said, very rarely will you have a completely flat surface to work with, so other areas of your rink will have more than 4" of water. So to calculate your initial fill volume, you'll need to use the average depth of your proposed ice slab in the calculation below. (For example, if you have a deep end of 12" and a shallow end of 4", and the slope is gradual, use a "thickness desired in inches" of 8".)

Rink width in feet × rink length in feet × (thickness desired in inches/12) × 7.48051948) = the amount of water you will need.

So for a 20'×40' rink with an average depth of 6", the calculation becomes: (20 × 40 × (6/12) × 7.48051948) = ~3,000 gallons of water.

For a 40'×60' with a shallow end of 4" and a deep end of 12", we'll use an average depth of 8" and the calculation becomes: (40 × 60 × (8/12) × 7.48051948) = ~12,000 gallons.

How long will it take to fill my rink?

Before I answer this question, I should explain that many people use water delivery trucks to fill their rinks. I am one of those people, mainly because my

house has a well and I don't want to tax the well pump while filling my rink. So while it's an added expense, it's nice to have 6,000-plus gallons of water dropped into my rink in about fifteen minutes.

If you're filling with a hose, the general answer is anywhere from eight hours for a smaller rink to several days for a larger rink.

For us math-nerds, the answer to this question depends on how much water you'll need (see above) and your hose's flow rate, which is measured in gallons-per-minute (GPM). To determine this, grab a 5-gallon bucket, your hose, and a stopwatch, and time how many seconds it takes to fill the bucket. Divide 300 by the number of seconds it took, which will give you your hose's flow rate. (For example, if it took you 45 seconds to fill the 5-gallon bucket, your calculation would be: 300/45 = 6.67 gallons-per-minute.) You can then enter your GPM result into the calculation below.

(Gallons Required/Flow Rate in GPM/60)

So if you're filling a 20'×40' with 3,000 gallons using a hose with a 6.67 GPM flow rate, your calculation becomes: 3,000/6.67/60, which equals 7.5 hours.

Should I fill all at once or in layers?

This one should spark some heated debate, because I know a number of people who fill in layers and end up okay. But with so many variables involved in rink building, I like to keep it simple, quick, and easy, so I fill all at once. Always have, always will. And here's why: Indoor arenas are entirely different animals than their outdoor cousins. Indoor arenas enjoy luxuries we can only dream about: no precipitation, constant temperature and humidity levels, a never-ending supply of water, a solid base of perfectly flat concrete, a grid of water-freezing glycol piping, and all the manpower and time necessary to make perfect ice.

For our outdoor rinks, we need to contend with the upcoming weather (be it snow or cold or warm temps), our schedules, and variable base layers and yard slopes, among other things. To treat your backyard rink like its indoor counterpart is to ignore any number of risks.

But before we get to those risks, let's look at exactly how indoor arena ice is made. Indoor ice is often only an inch thick in total and is applied in incredibly thin layers (1/32 of an inch), with some layers containing white paint or the lines, circles, and sponsors' logos. This process, even when done by professional icemakers, can take upwards of an entire day or more, and it requires very specific air and surface temps as well as humidity levels.

So let's transport that process over to our backyard rinks. I build my home rink on a tennis court, which has a slight slope starting where the tennis net would be to facilitate water runoff. When filled, my shallow end is at 4" thick and my deep end is at 8". It would take 256 layers of water at 1/32" to get my 8" depth in my deep end.

"But Joe, I've never put down *that* thin of a layer," you might protest. Okay then, let's say you put down an inch at a time, and your goal is to put it down in eight different floods. Your first inch goes in, and because you have a slope, it ends up all down in your deep end. You let it freeze there. Then you attempt to put in your second inch, only water doesn't sit nicely on top of your first layer (because it's subject to the laws of physics and thus designed to frustrate you), but instead finds its way *under* your frozen first layer. Because ice floats (consult a few ice cubes in a glass of water if you don't believe me), your first layer is now a giant floating ice slab with edges that are stuck to your liner. And as you fill each successive one-inch layer, your slab gets pushed up higher and higher, pulling on your liner and jeopardizing your entire season.

And that's not even the half of it. Who has time to fill for a week straight? What if you get a foot of snow in between layers but half your rink still has the liner exposed? What if your dog decides to hop in your shallow end and there's no ice there to keep his little claws off your liner?

In the end, there are too many risks. Want to avoid them? Fill in one go. If your rink fills in one go, and you time it in advance of some cold weather, by the morning after you are done filling you should have at least a protective coating of ice. Then within a few days you're skating, while your layer-loyal buddy is still putting in layer seven. He might eventually skate, and he might have no problems. But for

my time and energy, I'm dumping in a load of water before some cold weather and calling it a day.

Do I need to resurface every night?

I used to do this, and I know many of my customers do as well. To be honest, there's nothing wrong with going out and painting a new surface on your rink. It's just not necessary. Not by a long shot. When it comes to making good ice, the key factor is keeping the snow and ice shavings off of it, and for the most

part, I only whip out the hose to resurface when I know we'll be using the rink the next day. I always tell my customers and blog readers to plan ahead when it comes to rink maintenance.

What does that mean? For those of you who watch NHL hockey, think about how your favorite team works their goalie rotation. If the Bruins are playing a crummy opponent on Friday night and then facing off against the Red Wings on Saturday, you'll see them start their backup on Friday and keep their star rested for the marquee opponent the next day. What does this have to do with your rink? In the case of the Bruins, they made a decision on

Friday based on what was ahead. And when it comes to rink maintenance, you'll want to learn to do the same.

Let me explain. This is by no means the only way to do things, but it's how I roll:

IGNORE THE FIRST STORM IF ANOTHER ONE IS COMING.

If you clear a storm off your rink, but it's going to snow again within twenty-four to forty-eight hours, then just ignore it. Nothing good will come from spending twelve hours clearing off Sunday's storm, resurfacing seven times, scraping down the high spots, and purchasing a used Zamboni to make your ice perfect if it's just going to snow again on

Monday. Your sole job after a storm is to clear the snow off so your rink is exposed to the cold air. That's it.

UNLESS YOU'RE GOING TO SKATE, DON'T RESURFACE.

I mean, you certainly can, but you don't have to. I've had seasons where I resurfaced a total of less than five times. Note that when I say "resurface," I mean taking out the hose and laying down a coat of water. I *always* remove snow and skate shavings. But a true resurface? For me, that's like taking out your nicest suit; I only do it for special occasions. You can get pretty burned out on this rink thing if you try to battle Mother Nature and keep a perfectly smooth, indoor-quality ice surface every single day. Do yourself a favor and look ahead. Check out the upcoming schedule. Will it warm up? Will it snow? Am I leaving for a vacation or does my kid have a tournament? Then make your rink maintenance decisions based on that. You can get amazing ice quality by resurfacing daily, but I'd caution against striving for that unless you have nothing else to do with your time. You're no less of a rink builder if you let the rink sit there with bumps or cracks or imperfections during a busy week or if there is snow coming the next day.

I mentioned above that you should resurface if you're going to skate, and that's the exception to the "don't flood before a storm" rule. If it snows Friday, and we're getting another storm Sunday, but we're getting together for an EPIC SKATE PARTY with a bonfire and beer packed into the snowbanks on Saturday . . . you bet I'm pulling out all the stops on Saturday morning. Shoveling, flooding, scraping down bumps with the floor scraper, maybe another resurface—anything to get the ice perfect for the guests. Between Mother Nature and our hectic life schedules, when it all converges and we have a chance to throw a little bash, I make the ice as nice as possible.

What do I do when it snows?

In short, you get it off your rink as quickly as possible! There is a lot more detail on this in chapter 5 on rink maintenance.

Do I need special insurance for my rink?

There's no such thing as "backyard rink insurance," but we consulted with a number of insurance agencies and the general advice was twofold: Make sure you have a good homeowner's insurance policy, and then add to it with an umbrella policy. The standard policy typically covers injuries up to a certain amount, and then if there's a claim that exceeds that amount, the umbrella will kick in.

The other theme when talking to these insurance pros was to be up front and honest with your agent. Sure, you can hide your rink from your insurance company, but you could be in a tough spot if you have to file a rink-related claim without them knowing about it beforehand. Sure, there's always the risk that you tell your agent and they aren't crazy about the idea of a rink, but wouldn't you rather have that conversation in June and give yourself time to find another agency, as opposed to finding out in January when you need them to be there for you?

Of course, this is only my advice, and you should talk to your agent (and possibly your lawyer) about your specific situation.

CHAPTER THREE

Getting Started

Once you've decided you're going to build a rink, it's easy to get a little excited and want to run out and buy the first rink kit or pile of lumber you come across and start building. But while building your first rink isn't the most difficult project you'll ever undertake, I encourage you to be deliberate and to do the proper research and prep work to ensure success. Nobody wants to be the parent who has to sheepishly tell their kids that the rink isn't going to work because you rushed into it. Lucky for you, we're here to help.

This chapter will break down some of the rink-material choices you'll need to make, provide instruction on how to check the slope of your yard (which may be the most important pages in this entire book), and show you how to prep your yard for your frame construction.

Take your time and read this chapter carefully. Doing so will ensure that you make the right choices on materials and put the rink in a spot in your yard that will support it, all of which contributes to a positive rink experience.

Rink Liners

The liner is really the lifeblood of your backyard rink. You can survive shoddy board construction provided you don't have a huge slope, and you can get by with inadequate board support if you're lucky, but if you drop thousands of gallons of water into a liner that won't hold water, your season might be over before it even begins. So with that in mind, here are some rink-liner basics.

WHITE LINERS ARE BEST, FOLLOWED SHORTLY BY CLEAR LINERS.

I've used both, and both work well. It may not seem like it, but even in the dead cold of winter, dark things attract the sun. When your goal is to keep your ice hard and frozen, the sun is your enemy. So it would stand to reason that you would avoid those blue, green, or black tarps at the big home improvement stores, because your ice will be battling the sun all winter.

IF YOU CAN, USE ONE-PIECE POLY.

Nicerink, which makes the products we sell through Elite Backyard Rinks, makes 5-, 6-, and 10-mil-thick poly liners. Poly liners, in my experience, are your best option for holding huge amounts of water, because there are no places for the water to escape. Some folks buy multiple narrow pieces of poly and attempt to glue them together, and because water is so darn sneaky, it rarely works. Best to find a place that can send you custom-cut poly liners at the size you need. Sure, you can skimp on a liner, but don't come crying to me if it doesn't work in mid-December.

BUY A NEW LINER EACH YEAR.

Listen, I know it's no fun to shell out that money each fall. But my thought (and it's one I abided by even before I began selling liners) is that the world of outdoor rinks is dependent on so many things going right—temperatures, precipitation, your schedule—that I strive to be in control of as many variables as possible. And one of the easiest things to do is ensure you have a 100 percent solid, functional rink liner each year. Sure, you can attempt to reuse last year's liner—many do, some with success. But it's a risk, and for my time, I want to minimize as many risks as possible. So buy new each year. And if you're worried about the environmental impact of a liner, find a place nearby to recycle it, or use it to cover wood piles.

BUY THE RIGHT SIZE.

What size is that? The easy answer for folks allergic to math is to take your width and length and add about eight feet to each. So for a 30'×50' rink, you'd want at least a 38'×58' liner. Keep in mind it's impossible to add more liner once it's ordered and delivered, but you can always take a larger liner and cut it down. It's why I always add a few feet to each side for my rink customers.

If you want to plug your dimensions into a calculator, you can use this:

Liner Width = Rink Width (in feet) + Board Height (in feet) + 2

Liner Length = Rink Length (in feet) + Board Height (in feet) + 2

This gives you the bare minimum liner size with about a foot to spare on all sides. By all means go bigger if you can, but that's enough to hold water.

Boards

I've said it before and I'll say it again—there is no such thing as the "best" way to build a rink. Sure, there are ways that vastly improve your chances of success, and those are the methods we'll discuss in this book. Then there are those methods that really are not ideal, and we'll touch on these below. But as long as you can build what amounts to a shallow aboveground pool that holds water, you're in business.

RECOMMENDED BOARD OPTIONS

OSB PLYWOOD

This is the cheapest, flimsiest, and most easily attainable board material you can find. Found near the front of many home improvement stores, this material won't last you more than a couple of years. But I found it to be a great way to break into the rink world with minimal up-front investment. Thousands of my blog readers have used cheap OSB to build their first rinks, and the knowledge gained in the first year or two is invaluable when you finally take the plunge to a larger, sturdier rink design. If your slope will support it, then you can rip a 4'×8' sheet of plywood into one-foot strips and get 32 linear feet of boards for under $10. Can't beat that.

¾" PLYWOOD

A much thicker, sturdier, and more expensive plywood, ¾" will give you a couple more years over its OSB cousin. Made by gluing thinner pieces of wood together to form a strong multi-layered sheet, a sheet of plywood can be ripped into 2' or 1' boards, or kept intact for full-height boards. Be careful about offseason storage, as any moisture can get in between the layers and lead to significant warping. It's also not cheap, with ¾" sheets often priced at more than $30.

meaning you need a slope of 6" or less to use it. Iron Sleek sells a bracket that allows you to stack 2"×12" on top of each other, so there are options for yards with steeper slopes.

"TWO-BY"

"Two-by" dimensional lumber is thicker, sturdier, and will last much longer than either flavor of plywood mentioned above. Available in lengths anywhere from 6' to 16' and sometimes longer, the different lengths available at large lumber yards mean you can build a rink custom-fit to your yard without having to cut a thing, making your build quicker. That said, these long planks can be very heavy and difficult to store in the offseason because of their large footprint. But you can expect to get five-plus years out of a single board, making it a good choice once you know you're in it for the long haul. The downside is that the actual height of a 2"×12" is 11",

NICERINK BOARDS

We've installed north of eighty Nicerink setups in the last few years, and the genius of the Nicerink board is ever-present. Nicerink boards are made of a white thermoformed plastic, and come in 4'×18" size. The boards attach to each other using a male/female hinge system, allowing for radius corners, and the boards have indents that work with the Nicerink brackets. In the spring, you'll appreciate the stacking buttons that allow you to stack up your entire rink's worth of boards into a steady tower. It's not unheard of to stack an entire 20'×40' rink into a tower of parts with a 4'×18" footprint. After many revisions and changes over the years, the latest generation of Nicerink boards are nearly perfect, but it's hard to ignore the price, currently at $32/board. For even the smallest rinks, you're looking at over $800 in boards. The good news is that they'll last forever, and because of the quality, they're one of the only board options with a resale value.

WHAT WE'D AVOID

PVC OR ANY SORT OF PLASTIC-PIPE SETUP

There's one vendor, Ice N' Go, who sells its rink systems in just about every catalog known to man. It's almost hard to avoid, which is unfortunate, because the system simply does not work unless you have a perfectly flat yard (which almost does not exist). I have had dozens of people tell me that they tried the Ice N' Go, it failed, and they got so frustrated that they gave up trying to build a rink. As someone who is passionate about rinks, that drives me crazy. The system uses flimsy brackets and PVC piping to form the "boards," which the liner is draped over. I can see how that might work, but the reality is that it rarely does.

SNOWBANKS

This can work if your climate will support it—that is, you never, and I mean *never*, get a warm day all winter. When using snowbanks as boards, you're tempting fate with every 33-degree day. When it comes to rink boards, they serve two purposes: They give something for the liner to push against, keeping the water in, and they help with puck retention. When you're using snowbanks as your boards, best-case scenario, you have zero puck retention. You're simply hoping that the snow doesn't melt, so that your liner stays in place and keeps the water in. If it warms up and the snow melts, your liner will drop and your water will escape. Then it's bye-bye rink season. Best to try to get some sort of hard board in place that isn't so weather-dependent—unless you live in the Arctic Circle.

How to Determine the Slope of Your Yard

If you read one section of this book, let this be the one. This is the *single most important thing* every potential rink builder should do. This is step one. Your yard's slope allows you to determine your rink size, how tall your boards need to be, what kind of bracing you can use, how far apart you should space them, how much water you'll need, and what size liner to buy. When it comes to having the conversation with the spouse about building a rink in the first place, you'll have a higher rate of success if you know how much you're going to have to spend. Trust me.

You're going to need a few parts for this exercise, and because you don't want to spend a ton of money on fancy gadgets before you even know if your yard will support a rink, we're going to go old school and cheap. That means four things, maybe five.

MATERIALS AND COST

Wooden landscape/garden stakes at $10
A spool of string at $3
An inexpensive line level ($3 at a big-box store)

A standard tape measure at $10
Optional: a longer tape measure (100') at $5

Once you have these things, you're in business. Now let's take a look at your yard, and you'll have to be honest with yourself. It seems obvious, but you'll increase your chances of success tenfold if you try to keep your rink in an area of your yard that is relatively flat and does not have a significant slope. Sure, there are rinks out there with three feet of water in one end and four inches in another, but I wouldn't advise this unless you're prepared for the challenges that type of setup brings. Instead, my advice for your first rink would be to find a piece of property with no more than 6" to 7" of slope from one end to the other. If you're using 1'-tall boards, this allows you to have 4" of water in your high corner and up to 11" in your deep end.

STEP 1

Start by staking out your rink site. Using my advice above, eyeball a flat piece of property and follow some global backyard rink rules: Never build over a septic tank or leach field, try to stay close to the house unless you can snow-blow a path all winter, make sure you have access to a spigot and lighting, and make sure to plan the rink so that errant shots hit your neighbors windows, not yours. Basic stuff.

The first stake you should pound into the ground should be your shallow corner (the highest part of your rink, where you'll have the least amount of water). Every rink has one, and while you don't know the numbers yet, you should be able to visualize the highest corner. The idea is to plan on having 4" of water/ice here at a minimum. Then, using your tape measure (the optional longer spool tape measure helps with this step), pound in the other three stakes to create the four corners of your future rink. Getting the rink square takes a couple tries, so make sure you check your dimensions each time you add a stake.

When I'm doing a site survey for a customer, this is when I typically draw a rough sketch of the rink location and dimensions. You'll need this in a bit.

STEP 2

Take your spool of string and tie it around your high-corner stake 4" off the ground. This step simulates the water level at your high point.

On the sketch you created above, mark your high corner and write 4" next to it.

STEP 3

Now grab the spool and walk to any of the other three corner stakes and either attach it to the stake or hold it there. To make this easier if you're doing this yourself, you can drill a series of small screws into your non-high-corner stakes at one-inch increments. Regardless of method, the idea here is to pull the string taut between stakes so there's no sag. Then you'll take your cheap line level and attach it to the middle of the string. From here it's just a matter of moving the non-high-corner string up or down until the bubble in your line level is centered. Once

it is, take your smaller tape measure and, at the non-high-corner stake, measure how far the string is from the ground.

For example, if your string is tied to one stake at 4" and another at 10", this means you have a 6" slope between your high corner and this corner, and that once there is water in the rink, that corner will be 10" deep.

Repeat this step for the other two non-high-corner stakes, writing down the string height at each.

STEP 4

Take a look at your diagram. What you'll have now are board measurements and water heights for each of your four corners. Depending on what your string heights were, you may need to go through this process again. Was one corner 18"? You'll probably need 24" boards instead of 12" (not to mention a lot more bracing). Did you have a corner so high it was over the top of the wooden stake? Maybe bring the stake a bit closer to your high end and try again. Sure, your rink will be smaller, but you'll have fewer headaches if you can get the water level down.

STEP 5

If you're satisfied with your diagram and rink positioning within your yard, take a few minutes to measure how far your corners are from other features in your yard. Of course, you could always just leave the stakes in until you have your boards and brackets ready, but if that's not an option, you'll want a way to ensure your rink is in the same footprint as the four corners you just staked out. I typically measure the four corners from a non-moving item—fence post, pool, mulch bed, etc.

This is certainly not the only way to check level, but it's how I've done it on my rink sites and at customer sites many times. As long as your string is taut and your bubble is centered, this is a cheap and easy way to make sure you won't commit the single most common rookie rink builder mistake—having water pouring out over the boards at your deep end while the other end of your rink liner is bare. We've all done it, or at least come close. But take the half hour to stake out your rink and determine level, and know for sure that you'll be skating in December.

More of a rotary laser level kind of person? Awesome. The process is mostly the same (stake out your four corners and place the rotary laser tripod near the shallow corner), you're just measuring the laser height instead of the string.

How to Square Up and Prep Your Rink Site for Construction

No matter which rink construction method you choose, you need to make sure your rink site is square. Before you install a single board or pound in a bracket, aligning your four corners and getting your perimeters aligned evenly is essential. If you skip this step, you run the risk of your final corner not aligning or your liner not covering the entirety of your rink surface. We've seen it happen. To do this, you'll need four ground stakes (any kind will work), some string, a long tape measure (100ft is good), and some landscape spray-paint. For the dozens of rinks we build each year, this is our process:

STEP 1

Start this process by pounding in a ground stake, which we'll call S1. For my customers, I typically have a drawing of the yard and rink site that I did when I checked the yard's slope earlier in the year. When I do that drawing, I'll make sure to indicate how far away from the fence (or mulch bed or tree) the rink is. Then when I go back in the fall to build the frame, I make sure I put that first stake in the same spot where it was months ago.

STEP 2

Unspool your long tape measure to the length of the rink, and pound in your second stake, S2. This is the easy part. From the second stake, measure out the short side of your rink and put in your third stake, S3. So far, so good, right?

STEP 3

Attach the tape measure to S3, and walk it down to the area where you'll put in S4. But before you put S4 in the ground, continue walking back to S1. Depending on the dimensions of your rink, you'll want to let enough slack out of the tape measure to measure both the length and width of your rink. For example, for a 20'×40' rink, keep walking until you have the 60-foot mark showing on your rink. For a 30'×50', it would be 80 feet. Have a helper hold the tape measure at this mark, right next to S1, making sure the other end of your tape is still attached to S3.

STEP 4

To put in S4, grab your tape measure and walk out toward the perimeter of the rink until you are the correct distance from S3. For example, for a 20'×40' rink, find the 40-foot marker on your tape and walk out until the tape is taut. Since your helper is standing at S1 and keeping the tape at 60 feet, you know that when you pull the tape taut, you are 40 feet away from S3 and 20 feet away from S1.

LENGTH	WIDTH	DIAGONAL
20	40	44.7
24	40	46.6
24	44	50.1
30	50	58.3
40	60	72.1

STEP 5

Almost done! You now have a rink that measures all four lengths correctly. However, it still may be out of square. To check this, start with your tape measure at S1 and go diagonal across to S3, then note the length. A helper makes this easier. Then move your tape and measure the distance between S2 and S4. If the numbers match, then your rink is the right size and perfectly square. If the numbers are off, you will need to adjust the corners and re-measure your diagonals. Often this involves a bit of trial and error, and I always measure my lengths and widths before I start to build, to make 100 percent sure I'm ready to go.

STEP 6

Once my rink is measured out and perfectly square, I run some inexpensive string from one stake all the way around the other three stakes and back again. Then I grab a can of landscape spray-paint and trace a dotted line over the string. You *can* build a rink using just the string instead of the spray-paint, but I

find that it gets in the way. Once I've walked around the perimeter and sprayed my line, I re-spool the string and put it away for the next rink. At this point you can remove your four stakes. What you are left with is a sprayed line that shows exactly where to put your boards. Because you've checked your diagonals, you know your finished product will be square and will look great. You can now proceed with your build.

CHAPTER FOUR

Building Your Rink

You've checked your slope, noodled on material choices, and received the "go-ahead" from your spouse. There's no turning back now—it's time to build.

In spite of what others might tell you, my opinion is that there is no "best" way to build a rink. The best rink for you is one that you can afford, that fits your yard, and that gets your family out there and skating. There are dozens of combinations of parts available to rink builders, but what you'll read in this chapter are four common ways rinks are built. Once you get a feel for how these builds work, you can certainly go off-script and come up with your own plan using a combination of these (or other) materials. But if you're the type who prefers the step-by-step approach, then these four rink plans should work for you.

The plans below range from our inexpensive intro rink to a full Nicerink system to a DIY full dasher board rink. Some of these builds require specialized parts, others can be built after a single trip to the hardware store. Mostly, the plans below will show you how to build what I would consider to be entry-level-sized rinks. If you want to go larger, by all means, but you'll have to do a little math to ensure you have enough material.

So flip through the photos, get a feel for the work involved, and go build a rink that works for you!

Rink Plan 1:
The $250 Rink

What I'm sharing with you below is a rough approximation of my first backyard rink, the rink that gave life to my son's love for hockey, my family's connection to the game, hundreds of memories, and, in a roundabout way, this book. Tens of thousands of my blog readers have built rinks based on this set of instructions, and the low cost provides a testing ground of sorts. One year with this rink will tell you if you are ready to become a backyard rink family. It will also give you a taste of the maintenance and work involved in rink ownership.

This rink design is for a 24'×40' rink. The boards are 1' high OSB with wooden stake supports. (Note: if your slope measurements told you you'd have more than 10" of water in your rink, double your board height to 2' tall and put bracing every two feet around the perimeter).

For the boards, you're going to use 7/16" OSB sheathing. This is the stuff that the big-box hardware stores usually have near the front of the store. It's cheap, it's sturdy enough, and best of all, the major box stores will cut it for you. You will need four sheets of 4'×8' OSB, ripped into 1'-wide vertical strips. This provides you with 128 linear feet of board material, perfect for a 24'×40' rink.

In terms of supports, for my first rink I used 2'-tall wooden yard stakes. These are often found in the landscaping or building supply areas of your local home improvement store. You could also use rebar or 2"×4"s with one end mitered into a point, but we'll use the grade stakes because they're inexpensive and easy to use.

For a 24'×40' rink, you'll want a liner that is at least 28'×44', in clear or white.

There are also a few items you'll need to finish your install, but the cost is trivial and the pieces can be purchased anywhere. The first is a series of small metal mending plates, which you'll use to connect the boards to each other. Second, you'll need at least four L-shaped corner brackets to connect the boards. I used eight (two at each corner), and where the cost is relatively immaterial, I would recommend it. Lastly, you'll need screws to hold it all together. I suggest the stainless variety, or the type you use to build a deck. Make sure they're not so long that they're going to go through your boards and puncture your liner.

MATERIALS AND COST

Four pieces of 7/16" OSB sheathing at $7 each,
  or $28
Forty-two wooden stakes, $5 per six-pack, or $35
32'×45' liner, $150 shipped

Twelve board-connecting mending plates at
  50 cents each, or $6 total
Eight large L-brackets at $2.50, or $20
One box of exterior screws, $10

Total cost: $249

STEP 1
Start by staking out your four corners, ensuring that the rink area is square. See the section on squaring your rink site for details on that process.

STEP 2
Around the inside of your rink, lay out the 1' boards you had cut. Start in one corner, having a helper hold up two corner boards while you connect the boards using an L-bracket. From there, connect your boards to each other using the mending plates, making sure to keep the boards in line with the painted line you put down in Step 1. While you are connecting the boards, your helper can pound the ground stakes into the ground on the outside of the boards you have already connected. Start with 4' spacing between ground stakes, but go to 2' for areas where the water will be deeper. (Tip: Pound the stake 1'

into the ground, which leaves the top of the stake level with the top of your boards. Then drive a screw through the inside of the board into the stake.)

STEP 3

Continue until you have your entire frame built. Walk around and give the boards a little kick; add additional bracing where necessary. There is no such thing as too much frame support, but there *is* such thing as too little support. If it moves, support it with additional stakes.

On fill day, you can either use spring clamps or bumper caps to keep the liner attached to the top of the frame.

PRO TIPS

· Construction is much easier with a helper. Plan on some extra time if you provide beer or if the helper is one of your non-adult children.

· Whenever you use screws on a rink, make sure that the length of the screw is shorter than the thickness of the wood. You don't want the ends sticking out and injuring someone or damaging your liner.

· If you think you need more bracing, you do! Especially in year one, it's best to over-support your boards versus the alternative.

Rink Plan 2:
The 2"×12" + Rebar Rink

This rink is a bit sturdier, a bit more expensive, and will last a bit longer than the OSB-based rink from Rink Plan 1. Because 2"×12" are thicker and more resistant to warping and environmental damage, it's possible to get five or more years out of this setup, whereas you might get only a couple out of the OSB setup.

2"×12" are also a good choice because you can buy many different lengths without having to cut them. Most big home improvement stores will carry 2"×12" in 8-, 10-, 12-, and sometimes 14- or 16-foot lengths, meaning you can build a rink to suit your yard with minimal cutting.

Finally, because you can buy 2"×12" in such long lengths, using 2"×12" can be one of the quicker builds in this book. For this build, we're going to go with a 36'×48' rink. Keep in mind that the actual height of a 2"×12" is 11", meaning your slope should be no more than 6" or so.

MATERIALS AND COST

Fourteen 2"×12"s, $25 each, or $350

At least forty-two pieces of 2' rebar (you can purchase longer pieces and cut them with a chop saw to make it cheaper), $1.50 each, or $63

Pipe brackets to hold the rebar to the wood (one for each piece of rebar), $0.50 each, or $21

Corner bracing, $2 each, or $8

Large box of 1" screws, $10

40'x54' liner, $200 shipped

Total cost: $652

STEP 1

Referring to the section on squaring your rink, lay out and spray your lines. Once your corner stakes and string is put away, lay down your first board piece, starting at a corner. Have a helper hold the board upright while you pound rebar into the ground on the outside of your rink at 4' intervals. Attach the rebar to the rink using the pipe clamps and screws.

STEP 2

Where two boards connect, use a mending plate on the outside of the rink, screwing the mending plates from the outside of the rink in toward the inside. Be careful that your screws aren't so long that they stick out inside the rink, as this will puncture your liner.

On the corners, use a bracket on the outside of the boards.

STEP 3

Continue around the rink until you have formed the entire rink frame. On fill day, you can either use spring clamps or bumper caps to keep the liner attached to the top of the frame.

PRO TIPS

· Because 2"×12"s are very heavy, make sure you have a helper to build this rink.

· Rebar comes in different thicknesses and lengths. If you have a way to cut it (a chop saw), your money will go further if you buy a very long piece and cut it at home.

· In lieu of rebar, some big box stores will carry steel garden stakes. As long as you can get them in at least a 2' length, feel free to substitute these.

Rink Plan 3: The Nicerink System

With more than ninety Nicerink builds under our belt, I know more about this rink system than perhaps any other. And thousands of Nicerink customers around the world can't be wrong—Nicerink parts are among the most popular, most widely recognized backyard rink parts in the world, and with more than sixty years in the plastics industry, they're not going anywhere either.

While the price tag can be high for a new Nicerink, the quality of the parts and ease of installation make the price tag worth it if you can afford it. How easy is the install? For the most part, all you need is a dead blow hammer. That's it! No screws, no drill, no wood at all. And that's the genius.

The primary components of the Nicerink system are the white thermoformed plastic boards, the black triangular brackets, and their yellow foam bumper caps. Together with a liner, these are the only parts you need to be up and running with a top-of-the-line Nicerink system.

Nicerink parts can be ordered in two ways: through their website, Nicerink.com, and through their vast network of local dealers. For those in New England, we're one of them, but you can search for one in your area on Nicerink's website. The parts and prices will be the same, but you can often save money on shipping by purchasing from your local dealer, and they'll be right there to provide you with install services or support if you decide to build it yourself.

For this build, we'll show you how to build an entry-level 20'×40' Nicerink. Nicerink systems are modular, which means that if you want to increase size each year, all you need to buy are the additional boards, brackets, and bumper caps, plus a larger liner.

MATERIALS AND COST

Twenty-six Nicerink thermoplastic boards, $32 each, or $832

One Nicerink-in-a-Box kit (which includes 34 brackets and a 25'×45' liner), $315

Thirteen 8'-long Nicerink bumper caps, $10 each, or $130

Total cost: $1,277

STEP 1

Once you've staked out your corners and sprayed your lines as described in the square-your-rink section, you'll need to spray one more marker. At all four corners, 7'6" away from the corner, spray

a small marker to indicate where your corners will line up. We'll explain more below, but mark off these eight spots before you put the landscape spray-paint away.

STEP 2

With your lines in place, lay out your Nicerink boards around the perimeter of the rink. Once you do that, follow it up by laying out your brackets—aim for one every four feet if your water will be under 11" deep, or every two feet if it'll be deeper than that.

STEP 3

Grab a board and line it up on the sprayed line. Lay your dead blow hammer on the ground perpendicular to the board, then hold your fingertip where the

bracket and rock back and forth. It'll feel strange the first time, but it helps get the bracket most of the way in the ground. Then you can use your dead blow hammer to get it the rest of the way in, alternating between the front and back of the brackets.

STEP 5

We install the brackets and boards together as we go. So we'll install our first bracket, then slip the board into the opening at the front of the bracket. Then you'll line up your mallet perpendicular to the board, mark where the next bracket will go, push the board out of the way, and then install the next bracket. After that, you can install the next board, and so on. Do this all the way around the rink, only putting brackets in at 4-foot intervals, and only at the ends of each board.

bracket will go. Keep your fingertip there, but move the board. Now grab your bracket, put the front spike where your fingertip was, and align the bracket parallel to the mallet.

STEP 4

To install the brackets, you'll need to stand up and put one foot through the hole in the bracket. Using your mallet for support, put all your weight on the

STEP 6

If you need to put additional bracing in your deep areas, do that once the entire rink is done. To install the bracket in the middle of the board, line up your mallet perpendicular to the board, then disconnect one end of the board from the adjacent board. Swing the board out of the way and install the bracket parallel to the mallet. Put the board back into the opening at the front of the bracket and reconnect it to the adjacent board. Then continue on to the next bracket. I have found that building the entire rink using brackets four feet apart, then going back and adding brackets in the middle of the boards, is the most efficient way to build these rinks.

STEP 7

If your rink is approaching 15-plus inches of water, you'll want to brace the boards with a piece of 1" × 3" or 1" × 4" wood. There are notches at the top of the boards that will accept this piece of wood, and Nicerink will tell you to wedge that wood into the back of the bracket. We've cut these pieces of wood a bit longer and pounded them into the ground with success as well.

Rink Plan 4: The Full Dasher Boards Rink

Building full dasher boards is a bit more of a rink-building commitment. You're going to spend a lot more time building the rink, and the difficulty in storing full dasher boards means you may need to consider leaving this rink up year-round. That said, full dasher boards will give your rink the look of its indoor cousins, and the ability to rim pucks around the perimeter gives it the indoor functionality too.

I've been known to dissuade people from building a full dasher rink in year one. I've long thought that it makes sense to go cheap or simple in the first year or two so that you can get a sense of the maintenance involved, and so that you can ensure you'll use it enough to warrant the work and investment involved. But if you're ready to dive into the big time, here are the ways we've seen it done.

A few companies have popped up recently that offer full board kits that include the top rail, the white plastic facing, and the kickplates. But we're going to go DIY-style and show you how we've built

full rink boards using parts from your local home improvement store. For the quantities and costs below, we'll assume a 24'×40' rink. If you want to build a larger rink, just do the math to get the right quantities.

MATERIALS AND COST

Sixteen sheets of 4"×8×½" plywood (for the inside of the rink boards), $20 each, or $320

128 2"×4"×8" studs (for framing the boards), $3 each, or $384

Five large boxes of outdoor screws or framing nails, $10 each, or $50

40'×50' liner (larger so that it drapes over the boards), $175 shipped

Paint or stain, $50

Total cost: $979

STEP 1

Build your straight boards not unlike you'd build a wall in your home. Never built a wall? Follow along. A wall (and a rink board) is essentially a grid of 2"×4" lumber with a sheet of drywall (or plywood, for your rink) covering it. You're going to start with an 8'-long 2"×4" for your bottom rail and another for your top rail. Arrange them on the ground perpendicular to each other.

Because we're using a 4'×8' sheet of ½" plywood, we'll cut seven pieces of 45"-long 2"×4" to be our vertical studs. Why 45 inches? Because your sheet of plywood is 48 inches tall and your top and bottom rails are a combined 3-inches thick. Trust us.

Once you have your top rail, your bottom rail, and your seven studs, screw or nail the whole rig together. Starting on one end, and making sure that everything is straight and square, drive a screw or

nail through the top and bottom rails into the stud. Move 16 inches and add another stud. Continue until you're all the way through to the other side.

At this point you should have a nice little wall-like structure made up entirely of 2"×4"s. How do we turn this into a rink board? You slap a 4'×8' piece of plywood on it and screw it into your frame. Use outdoor-quality screws to resist the elements, and it's probably a good idea to either stain or paint it (using exterior paint, of course).

The end result is a solid framed board capable of withstanding both shots and the stray out-of-control body. Because this is a straight board, we'll use this behind the net and along the side walls.

STEP 2

Curved boards! Curved boards are beautiful and really give it that indoor rink look. And if you're like me, you've always wondered how you took the straight 2"×4" top and bottom rails and curved them. The trick? You don't use 2"×4"s. You use layered plywood.

Lay out a piece of plywood and decide the radius you want to use for your boards. You can always cheat and trace something that has the radius you're looking for. Then use a jigsaw to cut out four identical, curved pieces. Two will be glued or screwed together for the top rail, and two will connect for the bottom rail.

From there, you're building it just like your straight boards. Use 2"×4" for your vertical studs and screw a piece of plywood for the board surface.

STEP 3

Putting it all together! Join your beautiful new boards together using mending plates or by drilling holes in the outermost vertical 2"×4"s and joining the boards with a long bolt and nut.

To brace the board (and you'll still want to do that despite their bulk and weight), you can pound rebar through holes in the bottom piece of 2"×4", then attach 2"×4"s at a 45-degree angle to the top-half of the board to brace the upper board.

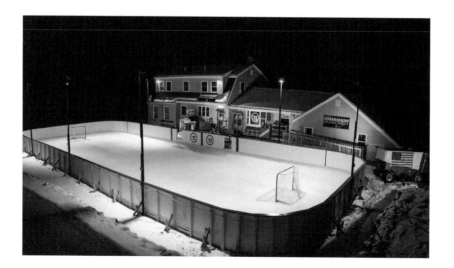

Fill Day! When and How to Lay the Liner and Fill Your Rink

You're almost there. You got the buy-in from your spouse. You measured your yard and bought the parts. You spent a day building your frame and making sure it was solid. Your kids have been doing a cold-weather dance for weeks, and now a cold front is approaching. Your dream has almost come true.

Fill day can be stressful, particularly for your first rink, but it doesn't have to be. It just takes a little bit of preparation and a deliberate, careful approach to laying out your liner. This is certainly something you don't want to rush through, and it's always a good idea to get help lugging the liner out to the rink site.

Once December arrives and you've identified the perfect fill window (see page 39), here's how to get the job done.

STEP 1

The first thing I do on a fill visit is take a walk around the inside of the rink. Sticks, branches, nails, screws, sharp rocks—all of it needs to be removed to provide the best environment for the liner. Anything sharp can potentially puncture your liner and lead to leaks.

STEP 2

Once the inside of the rink is clear of debris, lug your liner over and open the packaging. The liner label will often indicate if it should open length-wise or width-wise. With a helper, unroll the liner completely. Since your liner will be larger than your rink dimensions, take special care when unrolling it not to pull too hard near the boards to avoid the liner

getting caught on a board corner or bracket. You'll also want to make sure it's centered as best you can, both the long way and the short way.

STEP 3

Once the liner is spread out across your rink and draped over the outside of your boards, it's time to tuck it in. Start at one corner and adjust the liner so that it (a) is flush with the boards, (b) is flush with the ground, and (c) sits at a 90-degree angle where the board meets the ground. In other words, you want plenty of slack as opposed to having it stretched anywhere. To keep the liner in place, I typically use bumper caps, a yellow pool-noodle-style product that not only keeps the liner from moving but also acts as a safety barrier for falling skaters. You can also use spring clamps to keep the liner in place if you don't want to spend the money on bumper caps.

STEP 4

As you move slowly around the rink (a helper is . . . helpful), you'll undoubtedly end up with wrinkles in the middle of your rink. While you can walk on your liner (in socks, preferably), you'd be surprised at how easy it is to pull the wrinkles out from the perimeter of the rink. Small wrinkles that will fall beneath your water level can be left alone, but larger wrinkles should be pulled out. It may take a few tries to get the entire liner set up correctly, but it's important to get it in place before you start to fill.

STEP 5

From here, it's time to put the water in. Whether you have a fill truck delivering your water or you're using your garden hose, you'll have a few things to do while your rink is filling. First, you'll want to continually walk the perimeter and look for areas where the liner appears to be stretching. If you spot such an area, remove your bumper cap (or your spring clamp) and feed some extra liner from the outside into the rink. You'll also want to keep an eye on your bracing, particularly if it's your first year. Rinks don't typically fail when everything is frozen in January—they fail when the ground is still soft and you're introducing the tremendous pressure of thousands of gallons of water. It's why we always say there's no such thing as too much bracing, but there is such thing as too little. For new rinks, I recommend keeping some extra bracing on hand—rebar, wooden stakes, etc.—to put your mind at ease should you have some boards bowing out during the fill.

STEP 6

Once your rink has at least 4" of water in every area, you're done! Now all that's left is to wait until it freezes and enjoy it!

CHAPTER FIVE

Maintaining Your Rink

Owning a rink is not unlike owning a swimming pool—how adept you become at maintenance will determine the success of your rink. Green pool? No swimming. Rough, bumpy, snow-covered rink? No skating.

I've been doing this since 2008, and I still learn something new every year. Use the below as a guide, but be prepared to learn some lessons along the way. It's all worth it, I promise. And while it may seem that Mother Nature is conspiring against your skating plans, there are a number of things you can do to spite her. Below are a few fixes you can use to get your ice in good shape. This is by no means an exhaustive list of every possible scenario, as such an undertaking would never end. But it should at least get your ice in skateable condition in short order.

If you cannot stand on your surface . . .

In case you ever encounter a situation where your not-yet-thick-enough ice surface gets dumped on by snow, this is what will happen: First, the snow will weigh down your ice, pushing it downward. This will displace the water underneath, causing it to come up around the edges, mix with the snow, and create slush. This is among the worst of rink situations, but the solution is to do exactly nothing. If you're fortunate and your entire rink is slush, it should freeze relatively quickly. If you have snow on top of your slush, expect it to take a day or two longer to freeze, as the snow acts as an insulator. But you really can't do anything until the slush freezes and you can walk on it. Once that happens, see below.

If you can stand on your surface, and it snows . . .

Shovel it! The quicker you get the snow off your rink, the easier it will be to maintain a smooth surface. If you let the snow hang around for a while, it forms a bond with the ice, and even after you shovel, you'll be left with an ugly surface that will require a flooding. This is exacerbated when the snow is wet and heavy.

If you can stand on your surface, but it's full of significant bumps, craters, cracks, etc. . . .

The solution here is a process called "bucket dumps." Bucket dumps are reserved for when your ice is truly a mess, and when you need to fill in serious holes or footprints caused by walking through or half-heartedly shoveling slush. What you do is arrange a couple of garbage cans on your ice surface. Then drop your hose in one and fill it. Once it gets about halfway full, tip it over, then drop the hose in the second bucket. Be sure to move the buckets around to get 100 percent coverage. Let the bucket dumps freeze overnight before doing anything else.

If you can stand on your surface, and it's just a little bumpy . . .

Go out and buy yourself a heavy-duty floor scraper and walk or skate around the rink and chisel away at the bumps. It's an inexpensive and easy way to get the ice smooth.

If you can stand on your surface, and there are a ton of spots with thin ice that cracks when you step on it . . .

Then you have shell (or shale) ice. This is formed when you lay down a thick layer of water (sometimes after bucket dumps if it's very cold and too much water pools up) and the top layer freezes before the middle layer. If you have shell ice (and I've seen it take over an entire rink before), your best bet is to stomp all over it until it's broken, then flood using a garden hose. Don't go too thick or else you run the risk of creating shell ice again, but you want to break that thin top layer and then fill the pockets with new water that will hopefully freeze smooth.

If you can stand on your surface, and you want to fill the skate marks or small imperfections . . .

It's as easy as a resurface. Also known as "flooding," what you want to do is lay a thin layer of water down, similar to the backside of a Zamboni. You can purchase heavy-duty steel versions or you can make your own. For those of you who don't have a resurfacer, you

can still do it the old-fashioned way (letting water run from a garden hose while you hold it just above the surface), though it's harder to keep the layer thin this way. Here are some tips for a routine resurfacing:

- Be sure to rid your surface of any and all snow. Snow from storms, snow from skating—doesn't matter. If you try to use a resurfacer over snow, the snow will collect in the towel, clump up, and freeze into a ridge. If snow removal is impossible, then flood using the open end of a garden hose. You'll drop more water down, but the relatively warm water will melt the shavings and you won't have a towel to worry about.

- Many new rink builders make the mistake of flooding all the time. This won't hurt, but it's unnecessary. If your ice is smooth, and your kids skate for a couple of hours, as long as you get rid of the snow shavings, you'll be fine. The sun has the ability to smooth the ice out that next day, even in the coldest temps. You can flood, but don't feel like it has to be a daily chore.

- If you have access to warm water, feel free to use it. Again, not a requirement, but it does tend to make for better ice.

A few final thoughts . . .

Some tools that will help you keep good ice, this year and beyond: a resurfacer (either high-quality steel or DIY PVC); a shovel (I have a generic one from the big-box store as well as a 48" SnowPusher-Lite, which I love); a squeegee (a separate one is fine, but the SnowPusher comes with a squeegee on one end); a high-quality rubber hose (my go-to hose is a 100 percent rubber model from Goodyear and it never freezes); and a sharp floor scraper ($25 at the big boxes). Moen also makes a very nice hot/cold spigot that I had installed a few years ago. Not all of these things are mandatory, but the more tools in your arsenal, the more conditions you'll be able to take care of.

It's important to remember that your backyard ice rink will never be as perfect and smooth as its indoor cousins. Those rinks have controlled climates, no snow, and very pricey resurfacers at their disposal. And you know what? Who cares?! My family builds our rink so that we can get outside, enjoy our yard in the winter, get some exercise, work on skills, and HAVE FUN! You don't need perfectly smooth ice to do any of that. So let the kids go, let them smooth out the bumps with their skate blades, and start enjoying your investment.

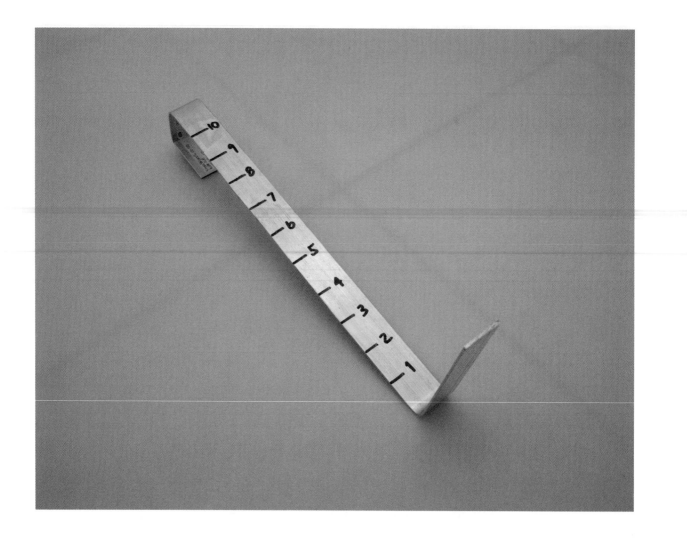

How to Make Your Own Ice Thickness Ruler

The necessity of an ice thickness ruler may not be obvious at first. In fact, I spent my first two years building a backyard rink without the ability to see how thick my ice was. For the most part, that inability was a non-issue. But one day in the middle of the 2009 season changed my mind.

It was January 3rd, and we were digging out from a three-day storm that saw nearly a foot of light, fluffy snow cover our rink. We had filled two weeks prior, so I assumed my rink was frozen to the ground, and that my liner was holding a solid brick of backyard ice. I was wrong—instead of a solid slab, my rink was merely a floating block of ice on top of a layer of water. The weight of the snow had pushed the slab down within my rink frame, displacing the water underneath and forcing it to seep up around the sides. This mixture of water and snow created a miserably heavy 2" layer of slush, the existence of which wasn't known until I planted a dozen size-12 footprints in it across the length of the ice surface. You

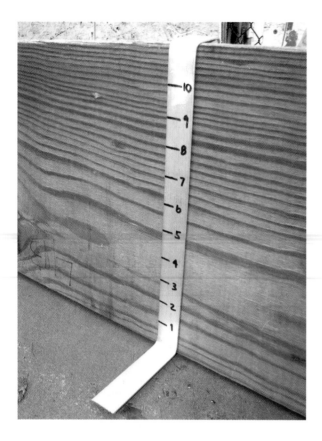

ruler is really simple. The only things you really need are a thin piece of metal, the ability to cut and bend it, and a Sharpie.

I absolutely cannot take credit for this design, as a member of the Yahoo! Backyard Rink group described it in an e-mail back in December 2009. When I e-mailed him and asked for his permission to include it on my blog, the e-mail bounced. So Rob (rbrand1124), if you're out there, the backyard rink community thanks you!

STEP 1

Your first step is to figure out how big your rulers need to be. The most important dimension of the ruler is the long middle part, which should closely match your board height, but you'll also want the bottom-most part of the ruler to stick out a bit. And you'll want to contour the top of the ruler to hang nicely over the top of your boards.

I found a bunch of metal strips in the hardware section of my local big box hardware store and purchased two pieces of 1/16"×1"×3' aluminum, which is flexible and won't rust. These particular pieces cost about $5 each. Cutting each piece in half will yield four rulers, one for each corner.

STEP 2

Once you know your sizes, it's time to bend the ruler into its shape. To bend the flat metal, I just used a block of hardwood and shaped the aluminum into a series of 90-degree angles. You want the ruler to hang on the top of your boards, stay flat against the

can guess what my dad and I did for the next two hours. My back still hurts.

Short of carefully shifting all of your weight onto the ice, it's rather difficult to see how thick your slab is. When you don't know if your rink is frozen all the way to the ground, it can affect your approach when you're trying to decide between removing snow during a storm or waiting until the last flake has fallen. And in the days following fill day, it also helps with the "Can we skate, dad? Can we, can we?" questions.

Lucky for us, the creation of an ice thickness

inside of the boards, and then jut out into the rink where the boards meet the ground.

STEP 3

Once you have the basic shape down, use a ruler or tape measure and mark off 1" (or 1cm) lines with a permanent marker, starting with 1 at the bottom and continuing up to the top of the ruler. To protect the lines and numbers, cover with a strip of clear hockey or packing tape. To protect the liner once the ruler is in place, take a dremel or piece of sandpaper and round off any jagged edges.

How do you use the ruler? It's easy. On fill day, lay your liner down and start to fill. Either before you put any water in or at least before any of the water freezes, put your rulers over the liner in each corner. Once you have ice, checking the thickness is as simple as lifting your ruler up. If it doesn't budge, that means your ice is frozen to the bottom. But if it lifts up, it will do so until the bottom of your ruler hits the bottom of the ice slab, and your ruler will tell you how thick it is. For some folks, this is hard to visualize, but for $5 in parts and under ten minutes of your time, it's worth it to try it out for yourself.

CHAPTER SIX

Disassembling Your Rink

You'll have to trust me on this one, but I'm writing this with a scowl. While everyone else will be giddy with anticipation over the approaching spring warmth, we rink builders are left with the saddest of sights: our new homemade reflecting pools. It was only weeks ago that these pools were host to family parties, neighborhood get-togethers, and intimate one-on-ones between fathers and sons. In the spring? Rinks are the world's largest birdbaths.

Not unlike death and taxes, springtime is something we must deal with every year. We don't necessarily have to enjoy it, but we do have to face it.

In this chapter we'll break down the essentials of the rink builder's springtime to-do list: the drainage, the teardown, and the storage of your backyard rink.

A quick side note on something I learned from my buddy Scott. Each spring, he takes a Ziploc baggie of thawed rink water and puts it in his freezer. Then each fall on fill day, he puts that frozen chunk of ice back into his rink—a passing of the torch, in some ways. I've done it for a few years, forgetting once in the spring of 2011. Of course, that fall and winter was our worst season ever.

Drainage

The godfather of backyard rinks, Jack Falla, had a saying: "Water seeking its own level will find it in your neighbor's yard." He learned this while attempting to fill his first rink at his parents' Massachusetts' home, but this adapted law of hydrodynamics applies to the end of rink season as well. To put it another way, if you want your kids to be able to cut through the neighbor's yard when they're late for the bus without getting vegetables thrown at them from the front porch, you'd better be sure you know where your rink water is going to end up. Ultimately, the dynamics of your yard will determine the approach you take.

For the first two years, our rink was situated in the middle of an old horse riding ring, off to the side of our property, relatively unused for anything else. Thus, it was easier for us to walk around in waterproof boots, slice holes in the liner, then just let the water saturate the unused earth for a week or so before going back out and getting the liner.

Our current house presents a bit more of a challenge. For one, our rink is situated on a tennis court, so there's really no place for the water to go directly beneath the liner. Second, the area immediately surrounding the court (where the water would likely end up) is usable yard that we'd like to keep from turning into a mud pit. So we now use a small, inexpensive submersible pump, which connects to a standard garden hose and acts like a sump pump to direct the water elsewhere. We have a sort of marsh toward the back of our property, which is easily reachable by a 50' hose. The rink will be empty, and my neighbors won't need waders to BBQ. Win/win.

You can also skip the pump and use a natural siphon if your yard slopes the right way. Siphons work by using hydrostatic pressure (and other big, intimidating words) to create a natural flow from one place to another. The catch is that the destination must be lower than the source. If your rink sits atop a plateau in your yard, and you have a drain or basin that sits down a hill, you might be in business. If your rink is at the lowest point in your yard, you may need a pump.

To start the siphon, place the hose (garden hoses are easier to use than large diameter hoses) into the rink, then place the other end where you want the water to go. You'll need to start the siphon by drawing the water out of the rink. An easy way to do this is to put the end of the garden hose inside the hose of a wet-dry vac. Taking care to seal off the junction of the different-sized hoses, turn on the wet-dry vac. Once water starts to flow, shut off the vac, move it out of the way, and watch gravity, hydrostatic pressure, and other neat phenomena come to life. With any luck, it'll drain itself.

Dismantling

Once your rink has been drained, it's time to dispose of the liner. If your rink is large, then your liner can be beastly. Don't try to fold or roll it up the way it was

when it was new. Instead, level the playing field with a pair of heavy-duty scissors or a utility knife. The goal is to slice your liner up in to manageable strips, which you can then roll up, tie into bundles, and dispose of.

Alternatively, if you're down with the green movement, I've heard stories of folks reusing old rink liners to cover boats or donating them to folks in need of large tarps. There are probably hundreds of uses for an old liner if you'd rather not throw it away.

Now that your liner is gone and your grass can breathe, it's time to think about the boards. Removal of your frame is optional, and is ultimately determined by (a) the summer plans for that area of your

yard and (b) your spouse's willingness to stare at what amounts to, regardless of the material you use, a warm-weather eyesore. ESPN broadcaster and backyard rinkmaster John Buccigross has been known to keep his boards up around his paved slab throughout the summer, giving his kids boards for roller hockey games. I wonder how many times a year he says, "But honey, it's for the kids!"

If you're going to dismantle, as I would, there is really only one rule: do it carefully and methodically. That might be two rules, actually. Because there are a million and one ways to build a backyard rink, there are also a million and one ways to dismantle a backyard rink. Before you grab the DeWALT cordless and go all NASCAR pit crew on the thing, take a moment to plan. Will you be setting up your rink in the same exact place next year? Did your boards fit together a certain way? If yes, take a half hour and number them. Once that's done, then the rest is just a bunch of reverse engineering. If you used screws in any capacity, be sure to have a container handy when removing them. Screws embedded in the grass are incredibly dangerous, both for the feet of your children and for next year's liner.

Storage

Another aspect of the backyard rink culture that often draws the spouse's ire is the storage of your frame pieces. If you're lucky, you have a spot in the garage, under the deck, or in the shed to hide them. Like dismantling your rink, storing it is unique to your situation. But there are a few things to consider:

- If you're going to leave your rig outside for the summer, as I have, know that the sun and elements will take their toll. Even if you don't have a structure in which to store your boards and stakes, covering them with a tarp (your liner, perhaps?) will at least keep them out of the rain. And unless your wooden boards are stained and sealed, you really don't want them soaking up water all summer. Indoor storage is preferable to outdoor, but if you must leave 'em out, at least cover them.

- Resist the urge to just stack everything on top of one another, particularly if it'll be stored outside (under the deck, for instance). Moisture from rain and humidity can get trapped between the layers, which will leave you a nice little penicillin surprise at the start of next season. I speak from experience. I used inexpensive OSB board for my first rink, and after stacking the pieces up one on top of the other, they were so moist and moldy that you could fold some of them in half. Your best bet is either to stand the boards up away from one another, or, if you must stack, to put a thin piece of 1"×2" or 2"×4" in between each piece to allow for air flow.

- Free pallets are pretty easy to come by and can work well as the base of your outdoor storage location. The pallet keeps the boards from the moist ground and serves as a stable base for the life-size game of Jenga you'll build on top of it. Remember to keep the air flowing between the sheets and to cover the top of your stack with a tarp or liner.

So there you have it. I've found that while I don't particularly enjoy the teardown of my rinks, it does help me turn the corner from cynical, cold-weather-loving outdoor hockey loon to normal, warm-weather-tolerating human being. Other humans seem to appreciate the transition.

CHAPTER SEVEN

Customizing (and Enjoying) Your Rink

Once your rink is built and the ice is in, there isn't much left to do other than to get outside and enjoy it. But in this chapter, we'll share with you a few things we've built to help enhance that enjoyment. From a replica of the US Pond Hockey Championship's wooden goals to the world's cheapest rink bench and a PVC skating aid that'll get junior up on his own *and* save your back, following are a few DIY projects to help kill the time between frame build and fill day—and some great ways to enjoy your rink when it's ready!

How to Build an Official US Pond Hockey Goal

If you're one of the thousands who spent time on the frozen bliss of Lake Nokomis this past winter, then you've heard it. Amidst the crowds and vendors and skates carving hard outdoor ice and huffs and puffs of USPHC participants, you've heard it. And if you've ever played pond hockey with a wooden goal, you can probably close your eyes right now and hear it clear as a Minnesota day.

It is, simply, "the plunk."

It is the sound of 6 ounces of black vulcanized rubber striking dimensional lumber, often the result of silky dangles, a laser-guided pass, or a long-range wrister. But however it happened, "the plunk" is one of the sweetest sounds in all of outdoor hockey.

With a half hour of your time and some inexpensive parts, you can have your very own wooden pond hockey goal to use on your backyard rink or pond. Thanks to our friends at the USPHC for the instructions.

May the plunk be with you.

MATERIALS AND COST

Thirty to fifty wood screws
72"×12" sheet of ½" plywood

Four 72"-long 2"×6" boards
Total cost: around $30

STEP 1

This is where you'll build the frame of the goal. You're going to start by taking a 72"-long 2"×6" board and attaching a 24" 2"×6" board to each end, so it looks like a giant letter "C." From here, you'll attach the crossbar, which is your 72"×12"×½" sheet of plywood. Lay that across the top and screw down into the frame. Bonus points if you decorate this piece.

STEP 2

He doesn't have much lateral agility, but he has absolutely no five-hole either. We're talking about your "goalie," or the wooden piece in the middle of your goal. Start with two 46" pieces of 2"×6" placed on the ground parallel to each other. Cut three 8.5"-long 2"×6" pieces and place in between, making a reinforced box. Screw it all together.

STEP 3

The reinforced box (aka, the goalie) gets centered under the crossbar and screwed into place with a half-dozen decking screws. Your pockets on the left and right should be about 12".

PRO TIPS

Get creative! I sprayed our blog name across the top of our crossbar, then stained the whole thing to withstand the elements. I also had some extra rubber floormat material, and screwed that to the backside of the goal frame. This protects the wood from repeated impacts (from my missile-like wrister, of course) but still provides that sweet, sweet plunk.

How to Build a $20 Rink Bench

Someone once called me a cheapskate. It was the nicest thing anyone had ever said to me. With that in mind, I present the $20 (or less if you collect used wood like me) rink bench. This design is battle-tested rinkside across the United States and Canada, and is the official bench of a handful of pond hockey tournaments. It's simple, it's cheap, and it'll keep your butt drier than sitting in a snowbank when tying your shoes.

I had about 90 percent of the parts sitting in my garage (and under my deck, and in my shed, and . . .) but if you bought it all from scratch, it would break down as such:

MATERIALS AND COST

Lumber: $8 or so. I used a pair of 8'-long 2"x4" and a single 8'-long 2"x6", but you could probably use four 8'-long 2"x6"s, which are typically under $2 each at the big-box stores.

Three 5-gallon buckets: $3 each. I went with two white and one blue, solely because they were the three I had that were the same height.

Mending plates or scrap 2"×4": free. You could buy these, but you can't tell me you don't have scrap wood lying around. More on exactly what you'll need below.

Hardware: $3. You're going to want six bolts, at least long enough to pass through the top of the bench and into the top of the buckets. 4" should work. You'll also want washers, one per bolt, and nuts to tighten it all up.

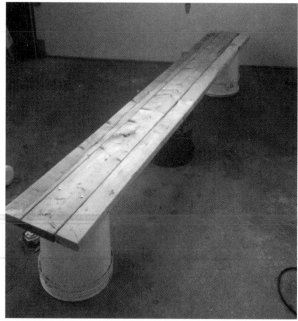

Here's how it comes together. If this takes more than a half hour, you're doing it wrong.

STEP 1

Start out by laying your wood on the ground, with the eventual bottom of your bench facing up. You can see this is all used, discolored wood, and ugly, though I prefer the term "rustic."

STEP 2

Your goal now is to attach the three boards to each other. There are a handful of ways to do this, and honestly, I used most of them. I had a couple extra mending straps, so I started with those.

Then I slapped on a couple pieces of mitered 2×4. I only mitered them so that they'd be less vis-

ible from the front, but you don't need to do that if you don't want to. It's not integral to the functionality of the bench.

And then a scrap piece of plywood for good measure. Hooray for having tons of crap in your garage!

STEP 3

Now you can flip your bench over and prop it up on top of the three buckets. Space them out evenly, then determine where you want to drill through. Since I put a 2"×6" as the middle of the bench, I marked the center of the 2"×6" then went 2" in either direction, such that both of my holes went through the 2"×6" and into the bucket. Drill slowly, as the plastic can break if you jam the drill down into it.

STEP 4

Once your holes are drilled, drop in your bolts. Then lay the bench sideways to put in the washers and nuts. I didn't use washers on the top of the bench, but used the largest ones I could find on the inside of the bench. I finger-tightened the nuts.

Flip it back over and you're done! Your very own super-luxurious, ultra-chic, "hey-honey-I-cleaned-up-that-scrap-wood-you-keep-bugging-me-about" back-yard rink bench.

I stained mine, but you could leave it alone, or cover it with chinchilla fur, or wrap it in old stain-washed jean fabric—the world, and this bench, are your oyster. No more wet bums from sitting in snowbanks, no more tying your skates standing up, and no more piles of scrap wood in the garage. Win, win, win.

How to Build a PVC Skating Aid

For all the joys associated with teaching a kid to skate—the shrieks of happiness, the "I'm doing it" look—there are certain pains as well. Namely the aches in your back and knees after spending two hours bending at the waist to hold onto tiny hands as they wobble around on miniature Bauers. So instead of volunteering your vertebrae to bear the brunt of Slugger's wobbly weight, why not drop $11 and fifteen minutes of your time and build a PVC skating aid? Bonus—your hands are free to hold the video camera.

MATERIALS AND COST

About 20' of 1-1/4" PVC
Six 90-degree elbows (Amazon)
Two 45-degree slip connectors (Amazon)
Four slip t-connectors (Amazon)
PVC cleaner and glue (Amazon)

Total cost: My receipt for the entire purchase was south of $12 using 1-1/4" PVC.

STEP 1

You'll need to cut the PVC into several lengths. For young kids (four to six years old), I used these sizes:

- Four pieces at 30" each

- Two pieces at 26" each

- Two pieces at 14.5" each

- Four pieces at 6" each

- Two pieces at 4" each

Don't be too freaked out if one is a slightly different length. I eyeballed most of my cuts and made them using a table saw that was not made for PVC. It still works.

STEP 2

From there, it's just a matter of putting all the pieces together to match the photos. The first time you put it together, don't glue it. This gives you the ability to ensure the size works for your little skater, and to get the hang of assembly without the worry that you did it wrong. Once you're confident in the size and assembly, feel free to take it apart one junction at a time and glue it.

And that's it! If you take your time, this should take a half hour to build.

PRO TIPS

· Experiment with different sizes or pipe diameters. My oldest is five, and his friends are the primary users of this, so the sizes above worked for me. But PVC is cheap, so play around with the design and build what works for you.

· Make sure you double-check the parts you're buying before you leave the store. Those PVC part bins always have rogue pieces that are the wrong size, or have threaded parts in with the slip connectors.

Backyard Rink Activities

The hard work is done and the stress is behind you. The cold weather is here and your ice is hard and smooth. But not unlike a shiny new gadget unwrapped on Christmas morning, you may be looking at your rink and saying, "Um, so what do I do with this now?" The answer to this question is as diverse as the rinks themselves, as how a rink is used for a family of high school hockey players will differ greatly from a family with some wobbly-ankled toddlers. But following are a number of ways we've used our rink since we first built it in the fall of 2008. And while there is no "right" way to use your rink, perhaps some of these will be helpful to you as you glide into your first season as a rink master.

Learning to Skate

For young kids, stepping onto the ice for the first time can be terrifying—especially in a group setting. When you take a child to a skating class, you're asking them to strap on all sorts of unfamiliar gear, then to leave their parents and join an unfamiliar coach underneath the blazing halogen lights and surrounded by boards and glass. It's overwhelming for sure, and not just for the young kids.

A backyard rink provides a retreat from all of that. With a rink in your backyard, learning to skate becomes a self-paced exercise, one that can take place whenever it suits you. You can turn the music up or down, you can skate under the sun or the stars, and you can see to it that your little Gretzky is as comfortable as possible while he or she tries to master a very difficult skill.

Of course, teaching them at home requires something the organized learn-to-skates have in droves: a little expertise. It's OK, we're here to help! How you teach your child to skate is a personal decision, but here are a few tips that will help you even if you can't skate yourself:

1) Dress them correctly. Whether you arm them in full gear or just put a helmet and elbow pads on them, make sure that they are warm and that their vitals are protected. I require hockey helmets with full cages on my rink for anyone under high-school age, and I put shin pads, elbow pads, and pants on my little ones, but it's your rink and your kid. Also, every new skater wants to use a stick. By all means

let them have fun, but I teach learn-to-skate without sticks at first.

2) Teach them how to fall, and make sure they know it's OK. Pull up some NHL bloopers on YouTube if you need to. But make sure they know that the correct way to fall is onto their knees. Of course, the next lesson is how to get up. To teach this, have them kneel on both knees, put one skate blade on the ice, put both hands atop their knee, and push off hard to get the other skate up. This step may take months, or they may get it the first time. Every kid is different. At our learn-to-skate sessions, I spend a good chunk of the first two weeks taking the newest skaters back and forth behind one of the nets, "getting our belly buttons cold" by laying flat on the ice, then getting up and waddling back to the other side to do it again.

3) Build a skating aid like the one on page 131. Not only will it save your back, but it also frees you

up to man the camera! Your child will be comfortable knowing that they can hold onto something, as the "freedom" of being on the ice by themselves can be terrifying at first.

4) One thing your child will learn when holding onto the skating aid is that moving their feet back and forth, as if they were walking, won't work (unless you're in figure skates—and you'll need to consult someone else to teach skating in those). In hockey skates, the toes need to be pointed outwards so that the ice catches on the inside of the skate blade, thus propelling the skater forward. So when your son or daughter is holding onto the skating aid, teach them to bend their knees slightly, point their toes out, and push their toes out and back.

5) Once they can scoot around with the skating aid, sometimes they'll be happy to just do that. But if their goal is to play hockey or skate without the aid, you'll need to enact some tough love. Take the skating aid out of their hands and move it two feet away. Ask them to walk or glide over to it. Once they can do that a few times, push it further away. Make it a game. Cheer loudly when they make it, then pick them up and hug them before putting them back down and doing it again.

Congratulations! You just taught a kid how to skate.

Improving Skills

For those rink rats who have to be manually removed from the rink for meals and bedtime, here are a few ideas to build their skills while keeping it fun:

1) Target practice! You don't need expensive hockey targets to do this. My oldest son spent three years shooting tennis balls and pucks at empty jugs suspended from the top of our net by string. I can still hear the unique "BONG" when he nailed one. A friend of ours recently filled up a dozen water balloons, tied them to the net, and let their kids rip shots to see who could pop the most. The kids thought they were popping balloons, but they were actually learning shot accuracy and power at the same time. Make it fun and different and the kids will do it for hours.

2) Skating and agility can be improved with a simple obstacle course. Use pucks, cones, sticks laid out on the ice, old car tires, nets, hula hoops, and anything else you can find to make your skaters zig, zag, and zoom around the ice. Have some competitive souls? Time them! Use the stopwatch app on your phone to see who is the fastest, and keep a leaderboard on the fridge. Handicap it so the younger siblings win every now and then. They're racing the clock, but they're also trusting their edges, improving balance, and increasing their body control. And they'll do it a hundred times in a row.

3) Just let them play! The best part about having a rink in your yard is the complete and utter freedom to do whatever you want. Trick shots, fancy moves, spin-o-ramas . . . ask any NHLer and they'll tell you

that much of their creativity came under the open skies on a rink or pond, absent of the coach's glare or the time constraint of a standard practice. If your kids have friends over, they'll try all sorts of things that would never fly in a real game or practice. They'll learn what works and what doesn't, and they'll expand their hockey horizons just a little bit more. All good things. And don't think your rink is too small; USA Hockey and many NHL and college teams are preaching the benefits of small-area games, or games where players are forced to make quick decisions and move with a puck in tight spaces.

Have a small rink and six kids fighting over the same biscuit? Congratulations! You have yourself a small area game.

Host a party!

One of my first customers emailed me after his family's first season with a rink. He wrote to tell me about how great it was that he was able to turn an unused piece of land in his backyard into such a gathering place for his family and their friends and neighbors. And with the addition of a fire pit and maybe some lights, he's absolutely right. For most folks, the flat part in their backyard simply gathers snow all winter and serves no other purpose. But plop a rink down on it and you have a place for everyone to gather, skate, roast marshmallows over a fire, and create awesome winter memories.

One of my rink customers hosted his January birthday on the rink last year. Fifteen kids played hockey for two hours, and they were enjoying themselves so much that we had to bring the pizzas and cake rinkside so they didn't have to get undressed. Once the candles were out and the frosting wiped from fingers, they were back at it again for another few hours.

These are just a few ways you can use your backyard rink. I've done all of the above with my family. I've also skated alone under a full moon, invited friends over for Friday lunchtime skates, and sat on our rinkside bench and just watched our kids laugh, smile, and fall. Building a rink can be a challenge, there's no doubt about that. But even if the amount of time you put into getting that ice ready dwarfs the number of hours you spend enjoying it, I can assure you that those hours on the ice will be something you and your family will remember forever.

Go ahead. Go build your rink.

RESOURCES

WEBSITES

backyard-hockey.com
backyard-hockey.com/forums
eliterinks.com
nicerink.com
groups.yahoo.com/group/backyardrink
howtohockey.com
d1backyardrinks.com
ironsleek.com
centericerinks.com
www.backyardrink.net

BOOKS

Home Ice by Jack Falla
Open Ice by Jack Falla

2x lumber (Dimensional lumber) – Known often as "2-by-12" or "2-by-10," rink builders often use it for their boards as it is thick, solid, and comes in different lengths.

Boards – Any material that helps keep your liner up, water contained, and pucks and bodies inside the rink.

Brackets (Bracing, Supports) – Anything that helps keep the boards upright. Wooden stakes, steel garden stakes, mitred 2"x4"s, Nicerink brackets, etc.

Bucket Dumps – An ice maintenance technique used for significantly damaged ice surfaces. You drop a hose in a bucket, let it fill up, and tip it over.

Bumper Caps – A Nicerink product, well known for its bright yellow color. Bumper caps keep the liner attached to the boards and offer a place to sit and a bit of safety in the case of a fall.

Corner Bracket – An L-shaped item, typically steel or aluminum, that helps keep the corners from bursting when a rink is filled.

Fill Day – The best day of the year! Fill day is when you place your liner down and fill it with water.

Floor Scraper – A must-have product. Found often in the flooring section of hardware stores, a floor scraper is a must for shaving down bumps and imperfections in your ice.

Frame – This is what you typically build in November, and consists of your boards and brackets.

Liner (Tarp, poly) – Commonly white or clear plastic, the liner is what holds the water inside your rink.

Mending Plate – A small, inexpensive piece of aluminum that is used to attach abutting boards to each other when building wooden rinks.

OSB – Oriented Strand Board, it's an engineered wood particle board made by combining adhesives with wooden flakes. It's the cheap stuff at the front of the big box stores.

Plywood – Often confused with OSB, plywood is actually created with thin layers of wood veneer that are glued together. For rinks, use the thickest sheet you can afford.

PVC – A popular and inexpensive plastic polymer, rink builders use PVC parts for a number of DIY projects, most notably the ice resurfacer and the skating aid.

Resurface (Flood) – The process of laying down a thin layer of water to refresh the ice surface.

Techniques might include the use of a resurfacer or by simply walking the rink with a hose.

Slope – The grade of your yard. When it comes to rinks, flatter is better. If you haven't checked your slope, you are asking for trouble.

Submersible Pump – A must for easy disassembly of your rink. These pumps drop right into your rink and connect to a garden hose, so you can direct the melted ice away from your basement and into a drain or low point in your yard.

ACKNOWLEDGMENTS

I wish to personally thank the following people for their help, not only in the creation of this book, but also for their role in helping shape its author.

To all the members of the Yahoo backyard rink mailing list, several of whom have gone from online "rink" friends to good "in real life" friends: Scott and Debbie Millin, Len and Jen Bruskiewitz, Alex and Megan Rogozenski, Glenn and Jenn Pinckney, and Bill Arnold. May your weather be frigid and your snowbanks full of cold beer.

To Jack Falla for teaching me that it's acceptable to talk about hockey and emotions in the same sentence, and his son Brian for the constant encouragement, feedback, support, and the wonderful foreword in this book. The world needs more people like the Fallas.

To all of my backyard-hockey.com readers, especially those of you who read and interacted with the site in its infancy. For everyone who submitted photos for use in this book, including Matt Proulx, Jason Gosselin, Doug Cline, Kevin Stow, David Beaudet, Chris Gower, Kevin Hobbs, Ian Murphy, Jon Frankel, James Kilmark, Chris Therrien, Chris Cross, Chris O'Reilly, Amy and Jay Bergeron, Anje and Eric Skora, Philippe Gaubin, Paul Auger, Richard Wood, Michael Bunton, Tony Lindeman, Eric Gruber, Todd Churchill of Reasonfortherink.ca, Steve Pailler, Chris Mader, Adam Grieco, Matt Brault, Stephen Walkauskas, and everyone else who has submitted articles, commented on or shared our posts, posted on our forums, and made our little blog such a great resource for those in our community.

To all of my Elite Backyard Rinks customers, many of whom I now consider friends. To Jim and his crew at Nicerink for helping us bring the rink lifestyle to our customers.

To Scott Crowder for the signage at his great events, and all the other pond hockey tournament directors who partner with us to bring outdoor hockey to the masses. To Carson Kipfer at NGIN for allowing us to use his pond hockey goal plans.

To Ann Treistman and Dan Crissman from The Countryman Press, the former for taking a chance on an unknown blogger and the latter for patiently holding that blogger's hand and answering all his questions over the course of the last year. To Allan Penn and Holly Schmidt at Hollan Publishing for dropping this project in my lap and letting me run with it—without you, this dream doesn't come true. And to Becky Thomas, who somehow helped me take a bunch of random thoughts and run-on sentences and turn them into a real book proposal.

To Jeff Vachon, for your help building rinks and your unwavering support of everything else I attempt, and Diana, for sharing Jeff with us during rink season (even when it was approaching your due date).

To my sister Sandra, for believing in me even when I don't deserve it, and for helping me with the blog's SEO back when I didn't know what SEO stood for.

To my parents, who got me on the ice as a toddler and let me stay on it into my 20s, despite the significant expenses along the way. For my dad, always a willing wingman for my crazy ideas, not the least of which was that first trip to Lowes to buy lumber for a backyard rink. Thank you for all you've done—for the rink business and for my family.

To my three incredible kids, RJ, Reese, and Ryder, for allowing me to pursue my dreams even if it means I put you to bed a little early so I can write the acknowledgements for my book at the 11th hour. I can't wait to see what the future holds for each of you.

And finally, to my wife, my high school sweetheart and my rock, for allowing me to dream big while still keeping me grounded in our crazy reality. I love you. UATW!

INDEX

Italic page numbers indicate photographs.

$20 rink bench, 126–129
$250 rink design, 70, 72–75
2/4 lumber, 128
2" x 12" + rebar rink design, 76, 77–79
3/4" plywood, 54

A
accessories
 hockey goal, 120, 122–125, 123
 ice thickness ruler, 106, 107–109
 rink bench, 126–129
 skating aid, 130, 131–133

B
boards, 50, 54–56
bracing, 35–36, 75, 78, 84, 97
Buccigross, John, 116
bucket dumps, 101, 103
buckets, 127–128
bumper caps, 75, 79, 81–82, 94, 97

C
corner brackets, 73
curved boards, 90

D
dasher boards rink construction, 86–90
disassembling process, 112, 113–116, 117–118
drainage, 114

F
Falla, Jack, 114
fill day, 39–45, 75, 79, 92, 93–97, 113, 121, 108–109
flooding, 103–104
floor scraper, 48, 102, 103–104
frame construction
 $250 rink option, 72–75
 2" x 12" rink option, 77–79
 board recommendations, 54–56
 dasher boards rink option, 86–90
 and the disassembling process, 115
 of hockey goal, 124–125
 ice thickness ruler, 107
 photographic illustration, 50, 53, 58, 64
 squaring up and prep, 65–69
 and storage, 119
 timing of, 32, 39–40
frequently asked questions
 fill day, 39–45, 41

frequently asked questions (*continued*)
  and frame construction, 39
  grass protection, 32–35
  insurance, 48
  and liners, 36
  rink maintenance, 45–48
  and slope, 35–36
full dasher board rink construction, 86–90, 91

G

garden hose, 97, 103, 104, 114
grass protection, 32–35
ground stakes, 65, 67, 74

H

hardware, 124, 127–129
hockey goal construction, 120, 122–125, 123
hydrostatic pressure, 114

I

Ice N' Go vendor, 56
ice thickness ruler construction, 106, 107–109
insurance, 48

K

Kaplan, Stanley, 24

L

liners
  the basics, 52–53
  and the disassembling process, 114–116

and the fill process, 39–40, 44, 93–97
  and grass protection, 32
  ice thickness ruler, 107, 109
  importance of, 36
  Nicerink brand, 81–82
  and rink boards, 56
  sizing of, 65, 73
  storage of, 119
lumber, 127

M

maintenance of rink, 99–104, 105
mending plates, 73–74, 78, 90, 127

N

Nicerink system, 55–56, 80, 81–84, 85

O

OSB (Oriented Strand Board), 54, 72–74, 77, 119

P

plywood, 54–55, 87–90, 124, 128
preparation, for rink construction, 63–64, 65–69, 66
price ranges, 18
PVC material, 56, 121, 132–133
PVC skating aid, 130, 131–133

R

reasons to build a rink, 17–29
  difficulty and expense, 18
  for memories, 19, 21–23, 29

for skill building, 24–27, 25
for social reasons, 20, 26
for stress relief, 28
rebar rink construction, 77–79
resurfacing, 45–48, 103–104
rink bench construction, 126–129
rink liners. See liners
rink maintenance, 45–48, 99–104, 105
rink plans, 70, 71–90
    $250 rink design, 72–75
    2" x 12" + rebar rink, 76, 77–79
    full dasher board rink construction, 86–90
    Nicerink system, 80, 81–84, 85
ruler construction, 106, 107–109

S

scrap wood, 127–129
shell ice, 103
shoveling snow, 98, 100, 104
siphons, 114
sizing liners, 52–53

skating aid construction, 130, 131–133
"slip" PVC connector, 132
slope
    the basics, 35–36
    and construction materials, 54–55
    and the drainage process, 114
    and the fill process, 44
    measurements of, 59–62
    photographic illustration, 58
    and rink construction, 72, 77
snowbanks, 36, 56
storage, 119
submersible pump, 114

T

tarp. See liners
"Two-By" lumber, 55

W

wet-dry vac, 114
wooden pond hockey goal, 120, 122–125, 123